"Joe Rigney's *Courage* is a bellwether, defining and defending a virtue that every Christian will need in abundance in our anti-Christian age. Rigney's book is a gem and a must-read. It is surely a book that I will be rereading often."

Rosaria Butterfield, Former Professor of English, Syracuse University; author, *Five Lies of Our Anti-Christian Age*

"In a world paralyzed by fear yet attracted to displays of conviction, boldness, and fearless action, there is an opportunity for the joyful virtue of Christian courage to shine. In *Courage*, Joe Rigney not only provides an explanation of courage and where it derives from but also issues a call to courage for the glory of God. It's fantastic. I pray God uses this little book to stir big things in the hearts of many."

Erik Reed, Pastor and Elder, The Journey Church, Lebanon, Tennessee; Founder, Knowing Jesus Ministries

"Take heart, Christian! As Christians in the West watch their societies increasingly turn against their Christian roots, this call is particularly relevant. Compromise and cowardice are contagious—but so is courage. With clear definitions, introductory forays into classical virtue theory, and inspiring examples drawn from Scripture, Narnia, and elsewhere, Rigney seeks to foster virtue for faithful witness to Christ. I am confident this book will do just that for many readers."

James R. Wood, Assistant Professor of Ministry, Redeemer University

"The apostle John tells us that the coward's portion is in the lake that burns with fire. That means that courage is not some optional virtue for a select set of Christians. All of us need godly courage to unflinchingly face the unique challenges and battles of our time. Joe Rigney helpfully shows us what courage looks like—in men, in women, in stories, and in our Savior—so that we can gain the stability of soul necessary to be courageous in every trying time."

Abigail Dodds, author, *Bread of Life* and *(A)Typical Woman*

"Joe Rigney has quickly become one of the pastoral voices I trust most for discernment and wisdom when thinking through any topic. His treatise on courage—which explains that bravery is a habit we learn by rightly ordering our fears and setting our minds on God's promises—demonstrates why. In a culture where arrogance is so often mistaken for boldness and recklessness for strength, Rigney offers practical advice on how to draw true courage from biblical wisdom. In his encouragement to preach about unpopular sins and his counsel on developing courage appropriate to one's sex, he demonstrates how much he himself possesses the virtue he is writing about."

Megan Basham, Culture Reporter, *The Daily Wire*; author, *Beside Every Successful Man*

Courage

Union

Growing Gospel Integrity

Michael Reeves, series editor

Courage

How the Gospel Creates Christian Fortitude

Joe Rigney

WHEATON, ILLINOIS

Courage: How the Gospel Creates Christian Fortitude

Copyright © 2023 by Joe Rigney

Published by Crossway
    1300 Crescent Street
    Wheaton, Illinois 60187

Portions of this book build on two previously published works: (chap. 4) Joe Rigney, "Giving the Gospel in the Midst of Mayhem," Cities Church, August 2, 2015, https://www.citieschurch.com/sermons/; and (chaps. 4–5) Rigney, "Courage for Normal Christians," Desiring God, November 7, 2021, https://www.desiring god.org/.

Cover design: Jordan Singer

First printing 2023

Printed in the United States of America

Trade paperback ISBN: 978-1-4335-8313-1
ePub ISBN: 978-1-4335-8316-2
PDF ISBN: 978-1-4335-8314-8

Library of Congress Cataloging-in-Publication Data

Names: Rigney, Joe, 1982– author.
Title: Courage : how the Gospel creates Christian fortitude / Joe Rigney.
Description: Wheaton, Illinois : Crossway, 2023. | Series: Growing gospel integrity | Includes bibliographical references and index.
Identifiers: LCCN 2022049153 (print) | LCCN 2022049154 (ebook) | ISBN 9781433583131 (trade paperback) | ISBN 9781433583148 (pdf) | ISBN 9781433583162 (epub)
Subjects: LCSH: Courage—Religious aspects. | Fortitude—Religious aspects.
Classification: LCC BJ1533.C8 R54 2023 (print) | LCC BJ1533.C8 (ebook) | DDC 241/.4—dc23/eng/20230223
LC record available at https://lccn.loc.gov/2022049153
LC ebook record available at https://lccn.loc.gov/2022049154

Crossway is a publishing ministry of Good News Publishers.

VP   32 31 30 29 28 27 26 25 24 23
15 14 13 12 11 10 9 8 7 6 5 4 3 2 1

Contents

Series Preface

GOSPEL INTEGRITY IS, I suggest, the greatest and most vital need of the church today. More than moral behavior and orthodox beliefs, this integrity that we need is a complete alignment of our heads, our hearts, and our lives with the truths of the gospel.

In his letter to the Philippians, the apostle Paul issues a call to his readers to live as people of the gospel. Spelling out what this means, Paul sets out four marks of gospel integrity.

First, he entreats, "let your manner of life be worthy of the gospel of Christ" (1:27a). The people of the gospel should live lives *worthy* of the gospel.

Second, this means "standing firm in one spirit, with one mind striving side by side for the faith of the gospel" (1:27b). In other words, integrity to the gospel requires a *united* stand of faithfulness together.

Third, knowing that such a stand will mean suffering and conflict (1:29–30), Paul calls the Philippians not to be "frightened in anything" (1:28a). He describes this *courage* as "a clear sign" of our salvation (1:28b).

Fourth, Paul writes:

> So if there is any encouragement in Christ, any comfort from love, any participation in the Spirit, any affection and sympathy, complete my joy by being of the same mind, having the same love, being in full accord and of one mind. Do nothing from selfish ambition or conceit, but in humility count others more significant than yourselves. (2:1–3)

Paul thus makes it clear that there is no true Christian integrity without *humility*.

The simple aim of this series is to reissue Paul's gospel-based call to an integrity that means living *worthily*, *unitedly*, *courageously*, and *humbly*. We need to recognize, however, that these four marks are not abstract moral qualities or virtues. What Paul has in mind are, quite specifically, marks and manifestations *of integrity to the gospel*. As such, the books in this series will unpack how the gospel fuels and shapes those qualities in us.

Through this little series, may God be glorified, and may "the grace of the Lord Jesus Christ be with your spirit" (4:23).

Michael Reeves
Series Editor

Introduction

A TEENAGER IS MOCKED AND REJECTED by his classmates because he holds to biblical teaching on sexuality and biblical standards of morality.

A husband and father wrestles with whether to continue in his present job or take the risk of starting his own company.

A wife faces another day with a harsh and emotionally distant husband.

A mother is diagnosed with aggressive brain cancer while pregnant with her third child.

A Christian employee faces pressure in his office to fly a rainbow flag in support of LGBTQ+ initiatives.

A pastor prepares a biblical sermon on a topic he knows will displease some in his congregation.

A missionary prepares to take his family to an unreached and unengaged people group that has historically been hostile to the gospel.

A new convert must decide how to tell his Muslim family that he has embraced Jesus as Lord, Savior, and Treasure.

Each of these situations is different, and yet each of them requires the same thing—courage. This is a little book about courage. My aim in writing it is not merely to describe a virtue but to foster it. And not just any kind of courage, but Christian courage. My aim is that in reading this book, your heart would be strengthened by grace to overcome your fears and face the dangers before you with gladness and joy.

The connection between courage and joy may not be obvious to you. But the Bible unmistakably links them. So let us begin by establishing this basic link between courage and joy by considering Philippians 1 and three key concepts that appear there: boldness, courage, and fearlessness.

The Setting

Paul opens his letter with a profound expression of gratitude and joy for the Philippians. This church has partnered with Paul in the gospel from the very beginning (1:5). This shared mission and fellowship gives Paul great confidence that the

Philippians will persevere to the end because God will finish his work in and among them (1:6). Paul's confidence is grounded in his deep affection for these saints: he holds them in his heart, he partakes with them of grace, and he yearns for them with Christ's own affection. His affection for them expresses itself in rich prayers—that God would multiply their love and knowledge, that they would love what is good and excellent, and that, in so doing, they would be found pure and blameless at the coming of Christ.

Following this greeting—which is distinguished by the total absence of correction or expression of concern—Paul then seeks to update the Philippians on his own situation. More importantly, he seeks to rightly frame his own imprisonment and sufferings for the Philippians so that they can wholeheartedly join him in the gospel mission. This is where our key words come into play.

Emboldened by Imprisonment

Paul begins by informing the Philippians that his imprisonment has surprisingly served to advance the gospel. This is deeply counterintuitive. We would naturally assume that imprisoning Paul would be a setback. Faith comes by hearing, and hearing by the word of Christ. And the word of Christ is heralded by apostles and missionaries like Paul. So how can imprisoning the missionary advance the mission? Paul gives two reasons.

First, everyone involved in the situation knows that Paul has been imprisoned *for Christ*. He has borne witness to Jesus, even in his imprisonment, so that his jailers are clear about why he is in prison. As Paul says elsewhere, while he may be bound in chains, "the word of God is not bound!" (2 Tim. 2:9). The word of Christ is being sown, and perhaps even taking root, among the imperial guard. And this, of course, makes sense to us. Paul has simply found a new mission field, so that even his imprisonment has served to advance the gospel.

But then Paul gives a second reason, and we are again faced with a counterintuitive reality. "Most of the brothers, having become confident in the Lord by my imprisonment, are much more bold to speak the word without fear" (Phil. 1:14). The brothers have been emboldened *by* Paul's imprisonment? This again puzzles us.

We might naturally assume that the imprisonment of the lead apostle would depress preaching—that the other brothers would grow quiet and muted because Paul is in jail. This is, no doubt, what the authorities intended. Make an example of Paul. Show the other Christians what happens when you stir up trouble with this so-called gospel. And yet, far from shrinking back into silence, the other brothers have been emboldened to speak. They are taking more risks, daring to teach what might land them in prison along with Paul. How is this possible?

At this point, Paul merely notes that their bold and fearless preaching comes from their (increasing) confidence in the Lord. Something about Paul's imprisonment has deepened their faith and reliance on Christ. Paul, of course, knows that not all of the newly emboldened preachers do so from right motives. Some are preaching Christ from envy and rivalry. They chafe under Paul's fruitfulness and want to see him taken down a peg. They hope that their preaching will harm Paul, that his afflictions will increase because of their ministries (Phil. 1:1–17). (How much do you have to hate someone in order to preach the gospel with the aim of harming him?)

But others—that is, those who are speaking the word from their confidence in the Lord—are preaching "from good will" (1:15). They preach out of love—for Paul, for the saints, for the lost, and for Christ. They see Paul's imprisonment as a divine appointment; they know he's there for the defense of the gospel, commending the good news about Jesus to the imperial guard, the Roman authorities, and all who would hear of it.

Paul is not concerned about motives; he simply rejoices that Christ is proclaimed. Whether in pretense or in truth, whether from envy or good will, whether out of rivalry or out of love, Paul wants to see the gospel advance. And he sees that advance happening through his own ministry in the prison, through the bold preaching of faithful brothers, and even through the insincere preaching of envious brothers. Paul rejoices *whenever* and *however* Christ is truly proclaimed. Full stop.

Honoring Christ in Life and Death

But this is not all that Paul rejoices in. He also rejoices in his coming deliverance. This deliverance, he is sure, will occur through the prayers of the Philippians and the help and support of the Holy Spirit. In fact, it's likely that Paul expects the Holy Spirit to uphold him in his imprisonment and affliction as an answer to the prayers of the Philippians. Notice how Paul describes deliverance: "It is my eager expectation and hope that I will not be at all ashamed, but that with full courage now as always Christ will be honored in my body, whether by life or by death" (Phil. 1:20). The deliverance Paul expects and hopes for is not merely salvation from physical danger. It may include such temporal salvation. But the deliverance he anticipates through the prayers of the Philippians is ultimately the perpetual honoring of Christ in his body, come what may.

Or we could put it the other way around. What would it mean for Paul to *not* be delivered? For Paul, to dishonor

Christ in life or death would bring shame upon himself, and he would not be delivered.

This is a gut check for all of us. Paul sees imprisonment and the possibility of death as a threat, as a danger. But it is not a threat merely because he might die. It is a threat because the prospect of pain, suffering, and death might lead Paul to dishonor Jesus in his speech and actions, in his living and his dying. Is that how we see our afflictions and suffering? Are we mainly concerned that the suffering end? Or, like Paul, are we mainly concerned that we magnify the worth of Jesus in the midst of our suffering?

We must press deeper into Paul's frame of mind here. What does he mean that "Christ will be honored in my body, whether by life or by death"? Consider the next verse: "For to me to live is Christ, and to die is gain" (1:21). The word "for" signals that Paul is explaining how he hopes to honor Christ by life or death. And sure enough, he immediately talks about living and dying. If we connect the two verses, we can draw these conclusions:

- Christ is honored in Paul's life when Paul's living is Christ.
- Christ is honored in Paul's death when Paul's dying is gain.

Now what does each of these mean? What does it mean to say, "to live is Christ"? How is it possible for death to be gain? The passage continues:

> If I am to live in the flesh, that means fruitful labor for me. Yet which I shall choose I cannot tell. I am hard pressed between the two. My desire is to depart and be with Christ, for that is far better. But to remain in the flesh is more necessary on your account. Convinced of this, I know that I will remain and continue with you all, for your progress and joy in the faith, so that in me you may have ample cause to glory in Christ Jesus, because of my coming to you again. (1:22–26)

"To live is Christ" means fruitful labor. It means Paul will remain in the flesh, on earth, working for the progress and joy in the faith of the Philippians and the other churches. His presence with them will provide ample opportunity for them to give glory to Jesus. On the other hand, "to die is gain" means that Paul desires to depart and be with Christ—which is far better than remaining in the flesh.

So, to bring the whole picture together, we can say this: Paul is in prison. He is facing the prospect of suffering, affliction, and potentially death. He might be released.

He might be executed. He faces an uncertain and painful future. And yet he rejoices because he is fully confident that God will deliver him. The same providence that made the gospel fruitful in prison will make Paul faithful to the end. Deliverance for Paul means that he will honor and magnify Christ in his body, no matter what comes, whether by release from prison and life or by execution and death. Christ will be honored in Paul's life when the aim of Paul's living is Christ—fruitfully laboring to increase the joyful faith of the Philippians. Christ will be honored in Paul's death if he receives death as gain because being with Christ after death is far better than every good thing he loses on earth.

And here's the relevance for this book: Paul calls facing life and ministry and suffering and death in this way *courage*. "Full courage" (1:20). Christian courage is a desire-driven, glad-hearted treasuring of Jesus as the greatest good in the face of looming danger or death. And such Christ-treasuring courage in the face of death magnifies Jesus.

Fearless in the Face of Opposition

We've seen the surprising *boldness* of Paul's brothers when he is imprisoned. And we've seen Paul's own Christ-treasuring *courage* in the face of death. The chapter ends with Paul inviting the Philippians to join him in this bold and courageous fearlessness.

Before exploring what Paul says, I should clarify what fearlessness means. Fearlessness does not mean an absence of all fear. After all, it's clear that we must fear the Lord. Moreover, many forms of fear are perfectly natural responses to pain and hardship. God has designed us to recoil from pain (whether physical or emotional), and thus fear (of pain, of death, of other loss) may be present in us without necessarily being sinful.

In understanding fearlessness, then, we might consider its opposite—fearfulness. To be fearful is to give in or be mastered by one's fears. It is to succumb to fear, to allow fear to guide and direct our actions. To be fearless, then, is to master one's fears. Fear may still be present (in fact, later I will argue that courage, at one level, *requires* the presence of fear). But the fearless man conquers his fear. It doesn't rule him; he rules it. Fear is there, but is not his master. With that clarification, we can return to Philippians 1.

After expressing his confidence that God will deliver him from death for the sake of his fruitful ministry and that, therefore, he will come to the Philippians again, Paul instructs them about what to do in the meantime: "Only let your manner of life be worthy of the gospel of Christ" (Phil. 1:27).

The language here calls to mind other places where Paul describes conduct that is in step with the truth of the gospel (Gal. 2:14), walking by the Spirit (Gal. 5:16), keeping in step with the Spirit (Gal. 5:25), and walking worthy of the calling to which we've been called (Eph. 4:1). In all of these cases, the idea is that there is a kind of conduct, a way of life, that fits, adorns, and expresses the truth of the gospel. Paul calls the Philippians to live such a worthy life.

He then goes on to describe what that worthy life looks like. He identifies three things he hopes to hear about the Philippians—three elements that make up the manner of life that is worthy of the gospel. First, he hopes to hear that they are "standing firm in one spirit" (or perhaps, "one Spirit"—1:27). Second, he hopes to hear that they are "with one mind striving side by side for the faith of the gospel" (1:27). Both of these highlight a kind of gospel-grounded unity and single-mindedness among Christians. In the first case, the unity is an immovable firmness. In the second, the unity is a relentless labor and pursuit. But the common thread is that the manner of life that is worthy of the gospel is one in which Christians stand and labor for the gospel *together*.

The third element concerns us most directly. Paul hopes to hear that the Philippians are not frightened in anything by their opponents (1:28). In other words, the life worthy of the gospel overcomes all fear of men. Such fearlessness is a sign of judgment for the church's opponents and of deliverance for God's people. Both of these—the judgment and the deliverance—are from God.

We may rightly ask why we should be so fearless in the face of opposition. Paul is ready with an answer: "For it has been granted to you that for the sake of Christ you should not only believe in him but also suffer for his sake, engaged in the same conflict that you saw I had and now hear that I still have" (1:29–30).

The source of Christian fearlessness lies in the recognition that God has given us two things: he has granted us to believe in Jesus and to suffer for Jesus. Both the faith that unites us to Christ and the suffering that comes from that union are gifts from God. Knowing that both are gifts steels us in the face of our enemies. Opposition to the church does not arise haphazardly; it is not random or arbitrary. It is a gift from God. Therefore, when we Christians encounter such opposition in anything, we do not fear. Such fearlessness fits reality and is worthy of the gospel.

Conclusion

Boldness. Courage. Fearlessness. These are the watchwords in Philippians 1. In the remainder of this book, my aim is to deepen our understanding of these words. What is courage? Where does it come from? What is its opposite, and how can we resist that? What is Christian boldness, and how is it expressed? And how is courage expressed differently in men and women?

But before turning to these deeper questions, I want us to see one more crucial element about courage in Philippians 1. It has to do with the connection between the growing boldness of Paul's friends, his own courage in the face of death, and his exhortation to fearlessness for the Philippians.

Recall the two surprises from the beginning of the chapter. The gospel surprisingly advances through Paul's imprisonment because his brethren are emboldened to speak the word without fear. And they are emboldened because Paul's imprisonment has surprisingly increased their confidence in the Lord. How does this work?

Here's the principle. Seeing courage spreads courage. Seeing boldness awakens boldness. Seeing fearlessness overcomes fear.

Paul is in prison, facing the possibility of his own execution. But he is not despairing or depressed. He is happy and hopeful. He does not view his imprisonment as a setback. Instead he views it as an opportunity for gospel advance. He preaches to his jailers and proclaims the good news about

Jesus to the whole palace guard. He seeks to make Jesus impossible to ignore among his captors. He wields the word without fear.

What's more, he expects to be delivered—meaning, he expects that God's Spirit will empower him to magnify Jesus, no matter what comes. Paul has a desire-driven, Christ-treasuring courage in the face of looming loss and death. For him, to live is Christ and to die is gain, and this reality works in him indomitable courage in the face of opposition, imprisonment, and death.

When Paul's brothers and fellow workers see his courage, their confidence in the Lord grows. Paul's courage is contagious. They catch it, and their courage grows. They are literally en*couraged* by Paul's courage. And because Paul's courage is rooted in seeing Christ as his greatest treasure, his brethren's confidence is not in Paul but in Christ. They are confident *in the Lord*. And their confidence in the Lord produces boldness in the face of opposition. They are em*boldened* by Paul's boldness and speak the word without fear in the face of opposition.

And the boldness of the brethren rebounds back to Paul and strengthens his own faith. He hears that they, inspired by his example, preach Christ sincerely, from love and good will, and he rejoices in the proclamation of Christ. His joy is so full that he even rejoices when he hears that his opponents are preaching Christ from envy and rivalry. Paul's joy abounds because Christ is proclaimed.

And then Paul tells the Philippians about it. He reframes his own imprisonment as an opportunity for gospel advance. And he reminds them that they are "engaged in the same conflict" he is. They have opponents. Paul has opponents. They have enemies and threats before them. Paul has enemies and threats before him. And just as Paul's courage encourages his brothers, so also Paul intends his courage and the courage of his brothers to foster fearlessness in the Philippians. Paul invites them to join him in his joy-driven courage. They must pray for him, as he prays for them. They too must walk in a manner worthy of the gospel. They too must stand firm together, strive for the faith of the gospel together, and fearlessly preach the good news together.

The lesson of Philippians 1 is clear. Courage is contagious. Boldness spreads. Fearlessness is infectious. And when these virtues are caught, Christ is magnified.

1

Defining Courage

CLASSICALLY, COURAGE (or fortitude) is one of the four cardinal virtues (alongside wisdom, temperance, and justice). When we speak of virtue or excellence, we mean the perfection of something, like a diamond that has been cut and polished to reveal its true splendor. When speaking of moral virtue, we're speaking of the perfection of the will. According to Jonathan Edwards, "virtue is the beauty of the qualities and exercises of the heart, or those actions which proceed from them."[1]

Virtue begins with desire. We start with a kind of inclination or disposition toward some good thing. When that inclination is activated and we move toward the

---

1 Jonathan Edwards, *Ethical Writings*, ed. Paul Ramsey, vol. 8 of *The Works of Jonathan Edwards* (New Haven, CT: Yale University Press, 1989), 539.

good thing, we call that *desire*, and when we arrive and possess the good we aimed at, we say that our desire has been gratified or fulfilled. If the thing we are after is really good, and if we repeatedly exercise that inclination, we can begin to speak of virtue. In other words, it's the regular, habitual exercise of good inclinations and desires that we call virtue.

Theologians frequently distinguish between God's common work and his saving work. We sometimes refer to God's common grace and his saving grace. Common grace is common to believers and unbelievers alike. Saving grace is given to God's people alone. Likewise, then, common virtues are common to believers and unbelievers alike. Uncommon virtues are specific to Christians.

And this is where the proper framework for thinking about virtue is important. Courage, like other virtues, is present, in some measure, among both Christians and non-Christians. At one level, courage, gentleness, prudence, justice and mercy, stewardship, forgiveness, patience, courtesy, generosity, temperance, humility, compassion, and faithfulness are all common virtues. And common virtues are *virtues*. It's good that they exist, and it's good to ask God for his common grace to produce such virtues among non-Christians. But they are not necessarily true virtues.

True virtues are virtues that God works in us by transforming us by the power of the Holy Spirit. In other words, true virtues are acts flowing from union with Christ. They are not simply good in a narrow sense, if we only consider human and earthly relations. They are good in an absolute sense, because they flow from faith in Christ and love to God.

Put another way, as we explore the virtue of courage, the animating principle matters—not just the external action, as important as that is. We believe that the life of the virtue—the dynamic principle that moves us to habitual action—really matters. It matters that God is the source, means, and end of our virtues.

It matters if we want our virtues to please God, because "without faith it is impossible to please him, for whoever would draw near to God must believe that he exists and that he rewards those who seek him" (Heb. 11:6).

Consider two passages from the Sermon on the Mount:

In the same way, let your light shine before others, so that they may see your good works and give glory to your Father who is in heaven. (Matt. 5:16)

Beware of practicing your righteousness before other people in order to be seen by them, for then you will have no reward from your Father who is in heaven. (Matt. 6:1)

In both cases, the virtue is performed before others—light shining and righteousness practiced. One of them is commended; one of them is condemned. There's a way of being seen by others that doesn't please God, and a way that does. First Peter sheds some light:

> As each has received a gift, use it to serve one another, as good stewards of God's varied grace: whoever speaks, as one who speaks oracles of God; whoever serves, as one who serves by the strength that God supplies—in order that in everything God may be glorified through Jesus Christ. To him belong glory and dominion forever and ever. Amen. (4:10–11)

When we serve, we serve as stewards of God's grace. He works in us what is pleasing in his sight. We serve in the strength he supplies, because the supplier of strength is the receiver of the glory. This is why Paul is regularly expressing the paradox of the Christian life: "I worked harder than any of them, though it was not I, but the grace of God that is with me" (1 Cor. 15:10). "I have been crucified with Christ. It is no longer I who live, but Christ who lives in me. And the life I now live in the flesh I live by faith in the Son of God, who loved me and gave himself for me" (Gal. 2:20).

And so, as we reflect on the virtue of courage, as we explore the habitual exercise of this good inclination, we want to ensure that God is honored as the source, means, and goal of our virtue. "From him and through him and to him are all things. To him be glory forever" (Rom. 11:36).

The Paradox of Courage

The present chapter focuses on the common virtue of courage. We begin with G. K. Chesterton. "Courage," he says, "is almost a contradiction in terms. It means a strong desire to live taking the form of a readiness to die."[2] This is true, not only of higher and nobler forms of courage but even of the earthly and quite brutal forms of courage.

> "He that will lose his life, the same shall save it," is not a piece of mysticism for saints and heroes. It is a piece of everyday advice for sailors or mountaineers. It might be printed in an Alpine guide or a drill book. . . . A man cut off by the sea may save his life if he will risk it on the precipice. He can only get away from death by continually stepping within an inch of it. A soldier surrounded by enemies, if he is to cut his way out, needs to combine

2 G. K. Chesterton, *Orthodoxy* (Chicago: Moody Publishers, 2009), chap. 6, Kindle.

a strong desire for living with a strange carelessness about dying. He must not merely cling to life, for then he will be a coward, and will not escape. He must not merely wait for death, for then he will be a suicide, and will not escape. He must seek his life in a spirit of furious indifference to it; he must desire life like water and yet drink death like wine.[3]

At the outset, then, we must recognize the paradoxical character of courage. All courage implies a kind of double vision, even a division, within us. On the one hand, there is the danger, the threat, the thing that provokes fear in us. On the other hand, there is the reward, the prize, the thing that we desire so much that we overcome our fear and face the danger.

Both the danger and the reward have objective and subjective dimensions. Objectively, there is the external danger—suffering, pain, affliction, death. This danger awakens fear in us, so that we subjectively are afraid. We naturally recoil from the pain; we seek to avoid suffering and especially death. Paul succinctly identifies both dimensions in 2 Corinthians 7:5, when he refers to "fighting without and fear within."

3 Chesterton, *Orthodoxy*, chap. 6.

Likewise, the reward has an objective dimension. Life, honor, the deliverance of those we love—all of these are set before us, on the other side of the danger. And just as the danger awakens fear, so these awaken desire. We want to live. We want to receive honor (or at least, we don't want to be shamed). We want to preserve the life and safety of those we love. And so, in the face of the danger, we resist the natural recoil—the impulse to run away or shrink back—and instead we press on. We press through. We take the risk. We endure the pain. We lose our lives (or at least risk them), in hope that we will save them (or the lives of others).

Crucially, courage always appears in the face of real danger. No danger near, no courage needed. More importantly, courage only appears in the presence of real fear. No *fear*, no courage. A man who, on a foggy day, ignorantly walks along the edge of a dangerous precipice is not showing courage. His ignorance insulates him from fear, and therefore from courage. Make him aware of the cliff, then the fear will rise, and with it, the possibility of courage.

Fear and Desire

So then, courage always involves a double vision concerning danger and reward, fear and desire. Let's think more deeply about the relationship between fear and desire. First, fear and desire are inescapable concepts. It's not a question of *whether* we will fear but *what* we will fear. It's not a question of *whether* we will desire but *what* we will desire.

Second, fear and desire both have to do with good things. We desire good things, and we fear the loss of good things. And these are often reciprocal. The goods we desire are the same goods we fear to lose. We desire to live, to make a living, to have a good reputation, to be healthy and prosperous, to have meaningful relationships, to live with purpose. Similarly, we fear the loss of life, of livelihood, of reputation, of health and wealth, of relationships, of purpose.

Third, fear and desire are matters of moral concern. In other words, there are things we *ought* to desire and *ought* to fear. This will require some elaboration.

In his lectures published as *The Abolition of Man*, C. S. Lewis introduces the notion of the Tao. This is his term for the objective rational and moral order embedded in the universe, or what we sometimes call *natural law*. Lewis demonstrates that a belief in the Tao, in the objective moral order of the cosmos, was common to all ancient cultures and civilizations. (He took the term *Tao* from Eastern religions precisely to communicate this universality; he wanted to avoid the suggestion that a belief in an objective moral order is somehow merely a Western, European, or Christian belief.) Here's Lewis:

> Until quite modern times all teachers and even all men believed the universe to be such that certain emotional reactions on our part could be either congruous or incongruous to it—believed, in fact, that objects did not merely receive, but could *merit* our approval or disapproval, our reverence or our contempt.[4]

Central to the Tao is the doctrine of objective value—"the belief that certain attitudes are really true, and others really false, to the kind of thing the universe is and the kind of things we are."

> Those who know the *Tao* can hold that to call children delightful or old men venerable is not simply to record a psychological fact about our own parental or filial emotions at the moment, but to recognize a quality which *demands* a certain response from us whether we make it or not.

4 C. S. Lewis, *The Abolition of Man* (New York: HarperCollins, 2001), 14–15.

. . . And because our approvals and disapprovals are thus recognitions of objective value or responses to an objective order, therefore emotional states can be in harmony with reason (when we feel liking for what ought to be approved) or out of harmony with reason (when we perceive that liking is due but cannot feel it).[5]

So then, attitudes and emotional states (such as fear and desire) can be right or wrong, moral or immoral. Lewis goes on to unpack the doctrine of objective value in terms of the principle of proportionate regard. This simply means that we should *value things according to their value.*

"Can you be righteous," asks Traherne, "unless you be just in rendering to things their due esteem? All things were made to be yours and you were made to prize them according to their value?" . . . St. Augustine defines virtue as *ordo amoris*, the ordinate condition of the affections in which every object is accorded that kind and degree of love which is appropriate to it. Aristotle says that the aim of education is to make the pupil like and dislike what he ought.[6]

5 Lewis, *The Abolition of Man*, 18–19.
6 Lewis, *The Abolition of Man*, 16.

And, we might add, to desire and not desire, to fear and not fear what he ought. So, to return to the question of fear and desire, we can now say that not only are fear and desire inescapable, but they are moral and they can be arranged in a kind of order or hierarchy. We can speak of ordered loves and ordered desires and ordered fears.

Levels of the Soul

Now we come to a fourth fact about fear and desire. Fear and desire are passions. Passions are the immediate, impulsive, and almost instinctive motions of the soul. They are our snap reactions to the way we read reality. We call them passions because we are *passive* in the face of them. They are not actions we take (though, as we'll see, we are responsible for them). Instead, they happen to us, fall upon us, arise within us. The Bible regularly speaks of fear falling upon people (Luke 1:12; Acts 19:17) or coming upon people (Luke 1:65; Acts 5:5) or filling people (Mark 4:41; Luke 2:9) or seizing people (Luke 7:16; 8:37).

Passions were classically divided into simple passions—desires for or aversions from certain things—and arduous passions—complex desires for or against things in the face of obstacles and difficulty. Simple passions include love, hate, desire, and sorrow. Arduous passions include hope, fear, daring, and anger.

While passions are movements of our souls, they are also closely tied to our bodies. That's why the Bible frequently refers to them as the passions or desires of the body and the flesh. "Let not sin therefore reign in your mortal body, to make you obey its passions" (Rom. 6:12). "The passions of the flesh . . . wage war against your soul" (1 Pet. 2:11).

But though passions are tied to our bodies, they are not automatic processes like digestion and breathing and growth. Nor, as we noted above, are they under our immediate control.

A picture begins to emerge of different levels in our experience as embodied creatures. Think of these like floors of a building. In the basement our automatic processes drone on—breathing, pumping blood, digesting food, and growing. These bodily processes are subrational and involuntary; they occur apart from any choices or decisions on our part. On the top floor is our intellect and our will, the level of reasoning and choosing. Then there is the middle level, the level of the passions. The passions are semirational and semivoluntary. They are snap reactions based on our quick judgments and perceptions of what is happening around us or what may happen to us. This middle floor we share, in some measure, with animals. Animals don't reason and choose as humans do. But they do recognize things as dangerous or desirable, feel fear or desire in response, and then react accordingly.

Fortitude and Daring

With this picture of a layered or tiered psychology, we can better understand the division or conflict that creates the possibility of courage. Lewis again is very helpful in *The Abolition of Man*. He notes that our desires, appetites, and instincts are powerful, so powerful that "without the aid of trained emotions the intellect is powerless against the animal organism."[7] Unchecked, our passions become strong enough to master us. Syllogisms and arguments, he notes, are insufficient to keep our nerves and muscles at their post in the middle of a bombardment. The intellect needs something more to govern the passions.

> We were told it all long ago by Plato. As the king governs by his executive, so Reason in man must rule the mere appetites by means of the "spirited element." The head rules the belly through the chest—the seat, as Alanus tells us, of Magnanimity, of emotions organized by trained habit into stable sentiments. The Chest—Magnanimity—

7   Lewis, *The Abolition of Man*, 24.

Sentiment—these are the indispensable liaison officers between cerebral man and visceral man.[8]

For Plato, this "spirited element," this liaison officer between the top floor of the intellect and the middle floor of the appetites, is the seat of courage. Courage is a kind of resoluteness of mind in the face of difficulty and hardship. The conflict we experience is between the passion of fear (at the middle floor) and our higher desire to cling to what is good (or to avoid what is evil). Courage is a habitual, sober-minded self-possession that overcomes fear through the power of a deeper desire for a greater good.

Courage, then, can manifest in at least two different ways. On the one hand, courage strains toward what is good in the face of risk or danger. It gives and hazards all in the face of uncertainty. We might call this risk-taking or daring.

On the other hand, courage clings to the good in the face of pain or pleasure. Courage resists the impulse to retreat or to flee in the face of hardship, difficulty, pain, even death. It also refuses to be drawn away from its post by promises of lesser reward. This we call fortitude or endurance.

8   Lewis, *The Abolition of Man*, 24–25.

Both of these expressions of courage appear in the passage from Philippians 1 we examined in the previous chapter. The manner of life that is worthy of the gospel includes both a "standing firm" (fortitude) and a "striving together" (daring). The latter suggests forward movement and progress. Daring takes the hill. The former suggests immovability. Fortitude holds the hill already taken.

In both expressions, courage avoids excesses on either side. Most obviously, courage is the opposite of cowardice. Cowardice shrinks back from danger. It succumbs to fear and therefore refuses to take risks, or retreats in the face of pain, difficulty, and death.

At the same time, courage is the opposite of recklessness or rashness. Courage is guided by reason and wisdom; it recognizes what should and should not be feared, and it keeps the bigger picture in view. Courage distinguishes between necessary and unnecessary risks. A man may risk his life for a thrill—scaling a cliff without rope or skydiving out of an airplane. Or he may risk his life to save others from danger—rushing into a burning building to rescue a child or going to war for his country. Thrill seeking may be a kind of daring, but saving lives at the risk of one's own death is courageous. The reason for the risk matters.

Conclusion

So then, we may summarize the general picture of courage as follows. Courage involves a kind of double vision. It attends to both the danger or hardship before us and the reward and good beyond. Courage arises in the midst of internal conflict in the face of external hardship. Fear of pain and desire for pleasure, aversion to evil and movement toward good—these tensions create the context for courage. Fear and desire are inescapable, and courage rightly arranges our fears and desires so that we fear what we ought and desire what we ought.

Courage is a stable habit of the heart that masters the passions, especially the passion of fear, through the power of a superior desire (or a superior fear). Desire for the respect of one's fellows (and fear of being ashamed before them) steels one's nerves in the face of physical danger. Or love for one's family conquers anxiety for one's personal safety, and we rush back into the house to save them from a fire.

Courage, seated in the chest, follows wisdom's guidance and subdues our passions. This is why, as C. S. Lewis says, "courage is not simply one of the virtues, but the form of every virtue at the testing point, which means, at the point of highest reality."[9] If we are only chaste or honest or noble

9   C. S. Lewis, *The Screwtape Letters* (New York: HarperCollins, 2001), 161.

when conditions are easy, then we are not truly chaste or honest or noble.

Courage takes risks in the form of daring without falling into the excess of recklessness. Courage endures hardship in the form of fortitude without succumbing to passivity or cowardice. And whenever we encounter genuine courage, we find it unmistakably beautiful and noble. It is a lovely virtue, one that all men admire.

Such is the general or common virtue of courage. But this book is not merely about the common virtue. It's about the Christian virtue. So how does this natural virtue become supernatural? What turns common courage into holy courage? To that question we now turn.

2

Biblical Courage

COURAGE IS A HABIT OF HEART and mind that overcomes fear by clinging to (or reaching for) what is good in the face of hardship, pain, and danger. These two elements—the reward or good and the danger or evil—are present in all forms of courage. And in the last chapter, we noted that there are various dangers and various rewards that we have to face.

Parents risk their own safety to save their children from harm. Soldiers overcome fear of death as they fight for their brothers-in-arms or for their people. Whistleblowers risk social stigma and ostracism in order to bring the truth to light. In these cases, physical pain, death, dishonor, and loss of reputation are faced because of a higher love for greater goods—family, country, honor. And all of these operate at the common or natural level.

To get to the supernatural level, we must bring in the notion of eternal and heavenly dangers and eternal and heavenly rewards. There are indeed eternal dangers, and there are eternal rewards. Biblical courage means clinging to and pursuing the eternal good in the face of all earthly dangers, from confidence that one has been delivered from the greatest eternal danger.

Our Greatest Danger

What is the greatest danger that any human being faces? Not physical pain or social ostracism or even death. The greatest danger we face is God. And he is a danger to us precisely because he is absolutely good. As C. S. Lewis reminds us:

> Some people talk as if meeting the gaze of absolute goodness would be fun. They need to think again. They are still only playing with religion. Goodness is either the great safety or the great danger—according to the way you react to it. And we have reacted the wrong way.[1]

For sinners, God is the supreme terror, and when we rightly understand our situation, we are right to fear. As the

1   C. S. Lewis, *Mere Christianity* (New York: HarperCollins, 2001), 31.

Scriptures say, "It is a fearful thing to fall into the hands of the living God" (Heb. 10:31). Jesus himself makes this point in seeking to rightly order our fears:

> I tell you, my friends, do not fear those who kill the body, and after that have nothing more that they can do. But I will warn you whom to fear: fear him who, after he has killed, has authority to cast into hell. Yes, I tell you, fear him! (Luke 12:4–5)

Here is the precise point we saw in the last chapter. We ought to fear certain things, and we ought not to fear other things.

And the fear of the holy God, who has authority to cast into hell, is a live issue for every human being. The Bible is replete with such warnings of our eternal danger. The wrath of God is coming "upon the sons of disobedience" (Eph. 5:6). Indeed, it is even now being revealed "against all ungodliness and unrighteousness of men, who by their unrighteousness suppress the truth" (Rom. 1:18–19). For the moment, God's wrath hands us over to "dishonorable passions" and "a debased mind" so that we practice and approve "all manner of unrighteousness" (Rom. 1:24–32). But there is a "day of wrath" coming when God will execute his judgment on human rebellion (Rom. 2:5). For the self-seeking and truth-suppressing, there will be wrath, fury, tribulation, and distress (Rom. 2:8–9).

And according to Romans 3, all of us are condemned.

> None is righteous, no, not one;
>> no one understands;
>> no one seeks for God.
> All have turned aside [and] become worthless;
>> no one does good. . . .
>> There is no fear of God before their eyes. (vv. 10–18)

We are all naturally "dead in . . . trespasses and sins . . . following the course of this world," led around by evil powers, living in "the passions of our flesh," carrying out the sinful desires of our bodies and our minds (Eph. 2:1–3).

In a word, "all have sinned and fall short of the glory of God" (Rom. 3:23). We are by nature children of wrath, and therefore we all lie before the greatest danger imaginable and ought to be overwhelmed by fear.

But God

"But God!" These are perhaps the two greatest words in the Bible. But God, in the richness of his mercy and because of his great love, has not left us in sin and death and under his wrath. The good news is that God himself has sent Christ to rescue us from sin and death and wrath.

Jesus Christ, fully man and fully God, lived a perfect and holy life before the face of God. More than that, he died in our place, as a substitute, as a wrath-absorbing sacrifice. The biblical term for this is *propitiation*, and it deals with our ultimate eternal danger. Our debt is paid. God's wrath is removed. Because of Christ's death on the cross for sinners, we can gladly say, "It is finished."

But not only did Christ die for us; he was also raised on our behalf, for our justification. He not only dealt with sin and wrath but, more than that, conquered death. Death has been decisively defeated. The resurrection of Jesus gives us a living hope so that we are delivered from the fear of death.

"But God."
"It is finished."
"He is risen."

This is the good news, and when we receive this news by faith, God declares us righteous in his sight. He justifies the ungodly by faith in his Son. We receive Jesus, and he's enough. All our sins forgiven. All his righteousness reckoned to us.

And being "justified by faith, we have peace with God" (Rom. 5:1). No more rebellion. No more enmity with God. No more threat of wrath or fear of being cast into hell. We are at peace with the living God, and it is no longer a fearful thing to fall into his hands.

This gospel is the fountain of Christian courage. It is the source of holy boldness and fortitude. And this gospel courage has two distinct movements—boldness before God and boldness before men.

Boldness before God

The gospel of God's grace and the doctrine of justification by faith alone produce a holy boldness before the face of God. Christians do not slink into God's presence. Because we have a great high priest in Jesus, we not only hold fast to our confession but also approach God's throne with confidence and boldness, knowing that it is a throne *of grace*, and God stands ready to lavish us with mercy in our time of need (Heb. 4:14–16).

We see the same exhortation later in the book of Hebrews:

Therefore, brothers, since we have confidence to enter the holy places by the blood of Jesus, by the new and living way that he opened for us through the curtain, that is, through his flesh, and since we have a great priest over the house of God, let us draw near with a true heart in full assurance of faith, with our hearts sprinkled clean from an evil conscience and our bodies washed with pure water. Let us hold fast the confession of our hope without wavering, for he who promised is faithful. (10:19–23)

The blood of Jesus makes us bold to enter the heavenly holy place. He is our great high priest, reigning over the eternal house of God. Our hearts have been cleansed by his blood, and our bodies have been washed by baptism in his name. And because of that, we have full assurance to draw near, to approach the holy God without fear, because he has promised, and he is faithful.

The apostle John similarly speaks of confidence and boldness before God. However, he directs our attention particularly to the coming judgment and the confidence that we can have today because of what Christ has done. He exhorts his readers to abide in Jesus "so that when he appears we may have confidence and not shrink from him in shame at his coming" (1 John 2:28).

A few verses later, John exhorts his readers to love others, not merely in word but also in deed (1 John 3:18). In doing so, we demonstrate that we belong to the truth, which reassures us when our hearts condemn us.

For whenever our heart condemns us, God is greater than our heart, and he knows everything. Beloved, if our heart does not condemn us, we have confidence before God; and whatever we ask we receive from him, because we keep his commandments and do what pleases him. (1 John 3:20–22)

Two scenarios are set before us. In the first, our hearts condemn us, most likely because we have remaining sinfulness. We know that we still do not keep God's commandments perfectly. Our consciences are pricked, and our hearts echo the judgment of God that we deserve nothing but condemnation. In that situation, our love for fellow Christians reassures us that we belong to Jesus and that, in believing in him, God abides in us through his Spirit (1 John 3:23–24). God knows this, even when we forget, and so his free justification of us is greater than our self-condemnation.

On the other hand, there are times when our hearts don't condemn us, when we are manifestly walking in the light and keeping God's commandments. In those cases, we have no fear of the coming judgment. We are confident before God, and like in Hebrews, we approach his throne and ask boldly for him to answer our prayers (Heb. 4:16).

Toward the end of his first letter, John again stresses the central connection between abiding in God and boldness before his judgment. When we confess that Jesus is the Son of God, we receive the love that God has for us and then return that love to him (1 John 4:15). In doing so, we abide in love and abide in God (which is the same thing, since God is love). And when God's love for us swells into a return love for God and an overflowing love for neighbor, God's love is perfected in us (4:17). And this perfect love drives out all fear, especially the fear of punishment (4:18). Instead, we have confidence for the day of judgment (4:17).

In 1 John and Hebrews, the message is the same. Because of what Jesus has done, we are delivered from all fear of coming judgment. We are saved from the greatest danger we face, and as a result, we have confidence to draw near to God. Charles Wesley captures the beauty of this biblical theme in the final verse of his famous hymn:[2]

No condemnation now I dread;
Jesus, and all in Him, is mine!
Alive in Him, my living Head,
And clothed in righteousness divine,

2 "And Can It Be, That I Should Gain" (1738), https://hymnary.org/.

Bold I approach th'eternal throne,
And claim the crown, through Christ my own.

Amazing love! how can it be
That Thou, my God, should die for me!

Courage before Men

Christian courage in the face of God's righteous judgment is a wonderful reality. It's why the gospel is good news. But the gospel does not merely create boldness before the throne of God. It creates courage and boldness before the threats of men. In delivering us from the greatest danger, it also delivers us from every lesser danger.

We hear the refrain echo through the pages of the Old Testament. Consider the words of Moses to the people in Deuteronomy 31. This is a time of generational and leadership transition. Moses has led the people for forty years in the wilderness. But he will not be leading them into the promised land. Times of transition are ripe with fear. What does Moses say to the people in such a time?

And he said to them, "I am 120 years old today. I am no longer able to go out and come in. The LORD has said to me, 'You shall not go over this Jordan.' The LORD your

God himself will go over before you. He will destroy these nations before you, so that you shall dispossess them, and Joshua will go over at your head, as the LORD has spoken. And the LORD will do to them as he did to Sihon and Og, the kings of the Amorites, and to their land, when he destroyed them. And the LORD will give them over to you, and you shall do to them according to the whole commandment that I have commanded you. *Be strong and courageous. Do not fear or be in dread of them, for it is the LORD your God who goes with you. He will not leave you or forsake you.*" (Deut. 31:2–6)

Consider next his words to Joshua in particular, as the leader:

Then Moses summoned Joshua and said to him in the sight of all Israel, "*Be strong and courageous,* for you shall go with this people into the land that the LORD has sworn to their fathers to give them, and you shall put them in possession of it. *It is the LORD who goes before you. He will be with you; he will not leave you or forsake you. Do not fear or be dismayed.*" (Deut. 31:7–8)

Consider next the Lord's own commissioning of Joshua later in the chapter:

And the LORD commissioned Joshua the son of Nun and said, "*Be strong and courageous*, for you shall bring the people of Israel into the land that I swore to give them. *I will be with you*." (Deut. 31:23)

Then, after Moses's death, the Lord reiterates his call and his promise:

No man shall be able to stand before you all the days of your life. Just as I was with Moses, so I will be with you. *I will not leave you or forsake you. Be strong and courageous*, for you shall cause this people to inherit the land that I swore to their fathers to give them. *Only be strong and very courageous*, being careful to do according to all the law that Moses my servant commanded you. Do not turn from it to the right hand or to the left, that you may have good success wherever you go. This Book of the Law shall not depart from your mouth, but you shall meditate on it day and night, so that you may be careful to do according to all that is written in it. For then you will make your way prosperous, and then you will have good success. *Have I not commanded you? Be strong and courageous. Do not be frightened, and do not be dismayed, for the LORD your God is with you wherever you go*." (Josh. 1:5–9)

Later, in the midst of the conquest, Joshua echoes these words to the people:

> And Joshua said to them, "*Do not be afraid or dismayed; be strong and courageous. For thus the LORD will do to all your enemies against whom you fight.*" (Josh. 10:25)

In each case, the exhortation and the argument are the same. Be strong and courageous, *for the Lord is with you*. This confirms what we've seen about courage. Courage is linked to strength, particularly to a kind of mental strength and emotional stability. It is a firmness of mind in the face of external threats and internal fears. And most importantly, biblical courage comes from knowing in our bones that God is with us and for us. Because he will be with us wherever we go, we need not fear our enemies. We need not melt before their might. Instead, we grow strong in faith and we act in obedience.

These words echo down through Israel's history. We hear them in the Psalms, as David seeks to strengthen the saints with song:

> *Be strong, and let your heart take courage,*
> *all you who wait for the LORD!* (31:24)

When David commissions Solomon to his great task—the construction of the temple—he echoes the words from Deuteronomy and Joshua:

> *Be strong and courageous. Fear not; do not be dismayed.* (1 Chron. 22:13)

> Then David said to Solomon his son, "*Be strong and courageous and do it. Do not be afraid and do not be dismayed, for the Lord God, even my God, is with you. He will not leave you or forsake you,* until all the work for the service of the house of the Lord is finished. (1 Chron. 28:20)

When King Asa needs courage to put away the idols of Israel, Azariah the prophet strengthens him against the fear of man with the promise of God's presence and reward:

> The Spirit of God came upon Azariah the son of Oded, and he went out to meet Asa and said to him, "Hear me, Asa, and all Judah and Benjamin: *The Lord is with you while you are with him.* If you seek him, he will be found by you, but if you forsake him, he will forsake you. For a long time Israel was without the true God,

and without a teaching priest and without law, but when in their distress they turned to the LORD, the God of Israel, and sought him, he was found by them. In those times there was no peace to him who went out or to him who came in, for great disturbances afflicted all the inhabitants of the lands. They were broken in pieces. Nation was crushed by nation and city by city, for God troubled them with every sort of distress. *But you, take courage! Do not let your hands be weak, for your work shall be rewarded.*" (2 Chron. 15:1–7)

When Hezekiah is surrounded by the armies of Assyria, he strengthens the hearts of his people with these same words:

And he set combat commanders over the people and gathered them together to him in the square at the gate of the city and spoke encouragingly to them, saying, "*Be strong and courageous.* Do not be afraid or dismayed before the king of Assyria and all the horde that is with him, *for there are more with us than with him. With him is an arm of flesh, but with us is the LORD our God, to help us and to fight our battles.*" And the people took confidence from the words of Hezekiah king of Judah. (2 Chron. 32:6–8)

Isaiah calls these truths to mind when he seeks to give courage to Israel in the face of her enemies:

> *Fear not, for I am with you;*
>   be not dismayed, for I am your God;
> I will strengthen you, I will help you,
>   I will uphold you with my righteous right hand. (Isa. 41:10)

Psalm 112 similarly highlights the courage of the righteous man who

>   fears the Lord,
> who greatly delights in his commandments. (112:1)

Such a man fears the Lord and therefore conquers all other fears.

> He is not afraid of bad news;
>   his heart is firm, trusting in the Lord.
> His heart is steady; he will not be afraid,
>   until he looks in triumph on his adversaries. (112:7–8)

Such is the firm, steadfast, and immovable heart of the one who trusts in the Lord.

Again and again, God's people are called to overcome fear—to face threats and dangers and uncertainty with courage—because God is with them and for them and will strengthen them and help them and reward them.

And note the uniqueness of biblical courage. Natural courage is a strength and resoluteness of mind that overcomes fear. Biblical courage is a strength and resoluteness of mind that overcomes fear *in the strength of another*. Biblical courage is a dependent courage. It leans not on its own strength but on God's provision. We heard it in Paul's words to the Philippians in the opening chapter.

Paul will be delivered from the shame of cowardice and able to magnify Jesus in life or death because of the prayers of the saints and the help of the Holy Spirit (Phil. 1:19–20). Paul's courage, like the courage of Moses and Joshua and David and Solomon and Isaiah and Asa and Hezekiah, is a divinely wrought and divinely dependent courage. What strengthens the chest of the Christian to overcome the passions of fear and anxiety is ultimately not his own resources and competence but the Holy Spirit of God, supplied through the prayers of God's people.

The Ultimate Model of Biblical Courage

Which brings us to Jesus. We have already seen that Jesus is the ground of our courage through the cross and in the resurrection. But not only is he the ground of our courage through his work; he is also the model of our courage in his work. Consider Christ's agony in the garden of Gethsemane.

Jesus is deeply sorrowful and troubled (Matt. 26:37). He prays in agony and sweats blood (Luke 22:44). He knows what's coming—horrific pain, scandalous mockery, the scorn of men. And behind and through and in it all, the wrath of God against human rebellion. In the face of such looming pain and death, his emotional agony and distress is perfectly appropriate.

And in his prayers, we witness Christ's full human nature, including the tiered psychology we discussed in the last chapter. "Father, if you are willing, remove this cup from me. Nevertheless, not my will, but yours, be done" (Luke 22:42). At one level—the lower level of the passions—Christ does not desire to run this race. His will and desire is for God to remove the cup so that he need not drink it down. And it is good and right and natural—not sinful—for human beings to recoil from such pain. And yet, at the deeper level—the higher level of his holy will—he asks for God's will to be done. He perfectly governs the passion of fear and distress and presses on in full obedience to his Father.

How does he do it? The book of Hebrews testifies to Christ's own double vision as he faces dangers and seeks rewards. The author invites us to consider Jesus, "who endured from sinners such hostility against himself, so that you may not grow weary or fainthearted" (12:3). Jesus does not faint in the face of hostility or grow weary in his obedience, despite the obstacles in his way. And we are to follow in his steps.

> Therefore, since we are surrounded by so great a cloud of witnesses, let us also lay aside every weight, and sin which clings so closely, and let us run with endurance the race that is set before us, looking to Jesus, the founder and perfecter of our faith, who for the joy that was set before him endured the cross, despising the shame, and is seated at the right hand of the throne of God. (12:1–2)

Jesus is the founder and perfecter of our faith. And one of the ways he perfects our faith is by being our model of endurance in faith. We look to Jesus. We consider him. And what does the author ask us to consider specifically?

There was a race set before Jesus. He faced the agony of the cross, with all its pain and shame. He saw the danger and the threat and the hardship, and he felt fear and distress in the face of it. But the internal fear in the face of the external danger did not lead him to turn aside or shrink back or faint.

Instead, he pressed ahead. He endured the cross. How? "For the joy that was set before him." He looked to the reward.

As he faced the "fighting without and fear within" (to borrow Paul's phrase from 2 Cor. 7:5), Christ steeled himself with the hope of glory. He knew his Father's infinite delight in him. "This is my beloved Son, with whom I am well pleased" (Matt. 3:17). He knew that he had come from glory and was returning to glory. He prayed as much in his high priestly prayer:

> Father, the hour has come; glorify your Son that the Son may glorify you, since you have given him authority over all flesh, to give eternal life to all whom you have given him. And this is eternal life, that they know you, the only true God, and Jesus Christ whom you have sent. I glorified you on earth, having accomplished the work that you gave me to do. And now, Father, glorify me in your own presence with the glory that I had with you before the world existed. (John 17:1–5)

His reward was returning to the glory he shared with the Father. But not just this eternal glory. Jesus was returning to the Father "having accomplished the work" he was given. The Father had given a people to Jesus, and Jesus would see to it that his people would be with him where he is, to see his glory and to be filled with his love and delight. Jesus had come to win a bride and invite her into the glory the Son and Father have always shared.

What strengthened the heart of Christ in the face of the cross was the infinite glory of God shared with a redeemed people for all eternity. That was the joy set before him. That was the reward that overcame every fear. That was the source of the courage of Christ.

3

Failures of Courage

A COMMON WAY TO GROW in the knowledge of a virtue is to consider its corresponding vice. In addition to commending the virtues themselves, the Bible often helps us grow in wisdom by showing us folly, in diligence by highlighting laziness, and in humility by revealing pride. Thus, reflecting on cowardice can give us clarity about courage.

What is cowardice? Cowardice is the failure to cling to the good in the face of hardship. It's a refusal to risk in the face of danger. It's a failure of nerve that seeks a shortcut or a quick fix to avoid pain. Timidity, fear, faintheartedness—all of these are the opposite of courage. Cowardice abandons its post in the evil day. It abdicates and relinquishes; it folds and flees. Fear makes us melt. It saps our strength, withers the heart, and weakens our resolve. That's what it means to be dismayed and discouraged.

But as helpful as definitions are, we often need stories to make the virtues and vices concrete. We need to see them in action so that we can imitate them or avoid them.

In the Garden

From the early chapters of Genesis, we see examples of fear, cowardice, abdication, and faintheartedness. When the serpent tempts Eve, Adam is "with her" (Gen. 3:6). Here is a moment requiring courage and boldness, fortitude and strength of mind. Instead, Adam is silent and passive. Rather than taking up a sword to drive the serpent from the garden, he abdicates. There is a dragon to be slain, and Adam flees. He withdraws. He goes along.

More than that, his initial passivity leads to high-handed idolatry. He listens to the voice of his wife rather than the voice of God. When she offers him the fruit, desire to please her trumps his desire to cling to the good and obey his Father. Rather than lead Eve with courage and fortitude, he abdicates and follows her into sin and ruin.

The fall unleashes shame, guilt, and fear on the first couple. They sow fig leaves to hide from each other. They hide from the presence of the Lord when he comes to meet them. Why does Adam hide from God? "And [Adam] said, 'I heard the sound of you in the garden, and I was afraid, because I was naked, and I hid myself'" (Gen. 3:10). Having sinned, Adam is full of fear. He shrinks back from God's presence.

And even when exposed by God, he doesn't stop hiding. He cowers behind his wife, blaming her for his failure. More than that, he blames God for giving Eve to him as his helper and bride. "The woman whom you gave to be with me, she gave me the fruit of the tree, and I ate" (Gen. 3:12).

From abdication to idolatry to deflection. From passivity to rebellion to blame shifting. Adam's failure to stand firm, his failure to cling to the good in the face of trial and hardship, plunges him and the human race into misery. His passivity grows into high-handed rebellion as he worships and serves the creature rather than the Creator. And then in fear, he hides from God and deflects the blame onto his wife and the God who made her. And in doing so, he establishes a dark pattern for others to follow.

On the Mountain

Consider Aaron at Mount Sinai in Exodus 32. Moses is at the top of the mountain, meeting with God. Aaron remains at the foot of the mountain, overseeing the people. These people are full of fear and anxiety. Oppressed for hundreds of years in Egypt, they have now been delivered by ten dramatic plagues. Pursued by Pharaoh, they find themselves trapped at the Red Sea, only to be saved at the last minute. After this, they face the wilderness and the threat of starvation and thirst (Ex. 16–17), and then the threat of wicked nations who seek to prey on them in their weakness (Ex. 17).

Through it all, Moses has been their leader. He wields the power of God against Pharaoh with the plagues. He stretches out his hand, and the sea parts. He strikes the rock with his staff and the water flows. When his hands are lifted up, the people of God prevail in battle. When his hands fall to his side, their enemies prevail. Moses, as God's prophet, has been the living representative of God's deliverance.

Then, at Sinai, Moses goes up on the mountain, and the people are distressed at his absence and delay. "We don't know what happened to Moses," they say (Ex. 32:1). And so they demand that Aaron make gods to go before them, idols to comfort them in their distress and anxiety.

And Aaron caves. In the face of the fearful demands of the people, Aaron has a colossal failure of nerve. He finds their distress intolerable and their anxiety contagious. He looks for the shortcut and the quick fix and does something abominable. Like Adam, he abdicates his leadership and falls into high-handed idolatry and rebellion. He fashions a golden calf with his own hand and displays it for the people as their god. He builds an altar before the calf and proclaims a festival, attempting to save face with some syncretistic nonsense: "Tomorrow shall be a feast to the LORD" (Ex. 32:5). His golden calf will supposedly represent the great "I AM" (cf. Ex. 3:14), the almighty Maker of heaven and earth.

And then, when Moses comes to confront him, Aaron faithlessly follows in Adam's footsteps.

> And Moses said to Aaron, "What did this people do to you that you have brought such a great sin upon them?" And Aaron said, "Let not the anger of my lord burn hot. You know the people, that they are set on evil. For they said to me, 'Make us gods who shall go before us. As for this Moses, the man who brought us up out of the land of Egypt, we do not know what has become of him.' So I said to them, 'Let any who have gold take it off.' So they gave it to me, and I threw it into the fire, and out came this calf." (Ex. 32:21–24)

From "the woman you gave me" to "the people you left me with." "It's their fault," says Aaron in essence. "I was just standing here minding my business, and out popped a golden calf." Abdication to idolatry to deflection. Same song, next verse.

And again, this is a failure of nerve, a failure of courage. The people's fear overpowers Aaron's resolve. He lacks the strength of mind and fortitude of heart to cling to God in the face of the people's agitation. He prizes their approval above God's holiness, and his courage melts in the furnace of the people's distress.

In the Wilderness

After the people receive the law and build the tabernacle as God's portable dwelling with them, they set out from Sinai to journey to the land that God has promised them. They do not start well. They complain about the manna that God has graciously provided them, so God buries them in quail and sends a plague upon them (Num. 11). Miriam and Aaron rise up in jealousy and oppose Moses, and God disciplines them (Num. 12).

Nevertheless, God remains faithful to them and won't abandon them, because of his promises to Abraham, Isaac, and Jacob. This section marks a transition in God's dealing with Israel. Up until this point, the people have largely been passive before the might of God. God has delivered them from bondage in Egypt, and he has done so with a mighty hand and outstretched arm. The battle in the book of Exodus has taken place between Pharaoh and Moses, between the gods of Egypt and the God of Israel. Israel's role has simply been one of beholding Yahweh's mighty deeds.

Now, in the book of Numbers, God calls Israel to a more active role in the next stage of his redemptive plan. Yahweh will go before them and drive out the nations, but the people themselves will be participants in the conquest. God directs them to send twelve men to spy out the land to see whether the people there are strong or weak, whether the land is good or bad, and whether they dwell in camps or fortified cities (Num. 13:17–20).

The spies return and report that the land is rich and beautiful, flowing with milk and honey. But the people there are strong, their cities are fortified, and there are even giants, descendants of the Nephilim, dwelling there. As a result, ten of the spies say, "We are not able to go up against the people, for they are stronger than we are" (Num. 13:31).

The report of the spies saps the strength of the people. They weep and grumble against Moses and Aaron. Joshua and Caleb exhort them: "Do not fear the people of the land, for they are bread for us. Their protection is removed from them, and the LORD is with us; do not fear them" (Num. 14:9). Here is a direct call for courage in the face of danger. And the people reject it. They call for the stoning of Joshua and Caleb.

Their fear and rebellion awaken God's anger, and he strikes them with pestilence and promises that none of that cowardly and rebellious generation will enter the land. Their bodies will fall in the wilderness (Num. 14:29), and their children will inherit instead.

At Mount Sinai, the distress of the people overcame Aaron's resolve. In Numbers, the fear of the spies infects the people. In both cases, the lesson is the same: Cowardice is contagious. Fear spreads like wildfire.

The law of God explicitly recognizes this fact. In Deuteronomy 20, God gives the people laws concerning warfare. In the midst of these laws, he says, "And the officers shall speak further to the people, and say, 'Is there any man who is fearful and fainthearted? Let him go back to his house, lest he make the heart of his fellows melt like his own'" (20:8). Fear does not just affect the one who is afraid. It spreads. It melts the hearts of others. It weakens and enfeebles a community.

But we must not let fear and cowardice fool us by their weak and faint appearance. The Bible is abundantly clear that such fear of man is wicked and rebellious, rooted in unbelief and hardness of heart.

When the people fearfully demand an idol to comfort them, God describes them as "stiff-necked" (Ex. 32:9). The people's refusal to enter the land is actually a despising of

God, holding him in contempt (Num. 14:11). It puts him to the test (Num. 14:22) and is fundamentally wicked (Num. 14:27, 35). It is accompanied by grumbling and complaining, much like the blame shifting and excuse making of Adam and Aaron. To complain is to blame God for one's predicament and to charge him with wrong. To grumble is to impugn his goodness and care. However pitiful it may look, such cowardice and unbelief is wicked because it fails to trust the promises of God and cling to him and therefore won't risk anything for his sake.

In Antioch

From the garden to the mountain to the wilderness, the story in the Old Testament is the same. Abdication, cowardice, and fear lead to idolatry and high-handed rebellion, resulting in deflection, grumbling, and excuse making. And the same dynamics appear in the New Testament.

In the book of Galatians, Paul recounts a defining moment in the history of the early church:

But when Cephas came to Antioch, I opposed him to his face, because he stood condemned. For before certain men came from James, he was eating with the Gentiles; but when they came he drew back and separated himself, fearing the circumcision party. And the rest of the Jews acted hypocritically along with him, so that even Barnabas was led astray by their hypocrisy. But when I saw that their conduct was not in step with the truth of the gospel, I said to Cephas before them all, "If you, though a Jew, live like a Gentile and not like a Jew, how can you force the Gentiles to live like Jews?" (2:11–14)

To understand this passage, we have to have some grasp of the social situation in the first century. For Jews in the first century, the fundamental division in the world is between Jews and Gentiles, those in the covenant and those outside. Of course, there are some marginal groups (like Samaritans), some unusual Gentiles (like the God-fearers in the book of Acts, who worship Israel's God but don't adopt the whole Mosaic law), and various subgroups within Judaism (Pharisees, Sadducees, Herodians, and so forth). But the basic division is Jew and Gentile.

Into that world comes the gospel, the good news that Jesus is the Messiah—Israel's King and indeed the Son of God—and that through his death and resurrection, he rescues both Jews and Gentiles from sin and death. And this good news, which fulfills the Law and the Prophets, scrambles that basic division. As a result the social picture in the first century is complex and confusing. Here is a sampling of the various groups in play:

- Unbelieving Gentiles, pagans and idolaters of various kinds.
- Unbelieving Jews, divided into various parties and groups.
  - One group of unbelieving Jews is particularly zealous for the Jewish law and its traditions. This group often expresses its zeal for God in persecution of other, less zealous Jews. This is the group that leads the persecution against the early Christians, whom they regard as unfaithful to the traditions of the fathers. Prior to his conversion, Paul himself was in this group.
- Early Christians, but with some distinctions among those who claim that name:
  - Jewish "Christians" who preach Jesus + torah, Jesus + keeping the Jewish law—especially circumcision and food laws—and expect Gentile Christians to do the same. This is the torah-observant and torah-preaching mission to the Gentiles. (This is the group causing trouble in Galatia.)

- Jewish Christians who continue to practice Jewish customs themselves but do not require Gentiles to do so.
  - Some, like Paul, do so only when engaged in evangelism to Jews (Acts 22; 1 Cor. 9).
  - Others likely do so out of habit and custom all the time.
- Gentile Christians who simply trust in Jesus for deliverance from sin and death without adopting circumcision and so forth.
- Gentile Christians who trust in Jesus and observe the full range of torah, including circumcision.

The situation is complicated. In Galatians 2, we see the results of interaction between these groups. Peter, the apostle to the Jews, likely continues to obey Jewish customs for the sake of his mission. But, because of the gospel, he gladly shares table fellowship with Gentiles in Antioch, as God showed him in his vision in Acts 10.

But then certain men come with a message from James. James is the leader of the church in Jerusalem. It's likely that his message concerns Jewish persecution of the early Christians there. We can imagine a message like this: "Peter, things are difficult for us here in Jerusalem. Our brothers and sisters are being thrown out of the synagogues. Some are being hauled off to prison for their faith. When the circumcision party hears that you're dining with Gentiles, it makes things very hard for us. Maybe you could stop eating with the Gentiles for a while? Until things settle down?"

And as a result, Peter draws back, out of fear of the circumcision party (either unbelieving Jews or the Jewish "Christians" who believe Gentiles must obey the whole Mosaic law). The rest of the Jewish Christians follow their leader—even Barnabas. Don't miss the word "even" in that sentence. We're meant to be shocked. Barnabas, the son of encouragement, succumbs to the pressure of his Jewish brethren and follows them into hypocrisy.

And so we see the same theme in this passage: fear spreads. Cowardice is contagious. Fear spreads from Peter to the Jews to Barnabas and threatens to wreak havoc on the fledgling church.

More than that, this story highlights a key element of the way fear and pressure work. Those closest to us are often the greatest threat to our courage and fortitude. Eve influenced Adam to fall away. The people of Israel pressured Aaron. The spies—leaders from the twelve tribes—melted the hearts of the people. And the men from James infected Peter with fear, which then spread to Barnabas and the rest.

But not everyone. Paul sees the implications of this fearful act. He sees how withdrawing from fellowship with Gentiles out of cowardice tells lies about Christ and the gospel. The dividing wall separating Jew and Gentile has been torn down; everyone is justified by grace and through faith. Therefore, we must not rebuild that dividing wall out of fear. Paul stands firm in the truth. He is no pleaser of men but a servant of Christ (Gal. 1:10).

And so Paul confronts Peter and publicly opposes him, reminding him of their common Christian confession and the truth of the gospel of God's grace (Gal. 2:15–21). And though Paul doesn't record Peter's response in his letter to the Galatians, Acts 15 testifies to Peter's full acceptance of the Gentiles and his staunch resistance to the false brothers who would require them to be circumcised (15:5–11). It would seem that not only cowardice but courage is contagious as well.

Conclusion

So then, fear and cowardice are not small sins. Cowardice is a kind of rebellion, rooted in unbelief and the hardness of heart. It is contagious and, if left unchecked, spreads throughout a community and melts the hearts of all within it. But courage spreads the same way. It's infectious.

Hebrews 3 testifies to the danger of fear of man and hard-heartedness and the need for encouragement and confidence in the gospel. The author quotes Psalm 95, which is a psalm reflecting on the cowardly and rebellious wilderness generation:

Therefore, as the Holy Spirit says,

"Today, if you hear his voice,
do not harden your hearts as in the rebellion,
    on the day of testing in the wilderness,
where your fathers put me to the test
    and saw my works for forty years.
Therefore I was provoked with that generation,
and said, 'They always go astray in their heart;
    they have not known my ways.'
As I swore in my wrath,
    'They shall not enter my rest.'" (Heb. 3:7–11)

All of our themes are here: the fearful and fainthearted wilderness generation, with hard hearts, testing God, provoking him and going astray, and so suffering the consequences of their cowardice. And then the author of Hebrews draws the lesson:

Take care, brothers, lest there be in any of you an evil, unbelieving heart, leading you to fall away from the living God. But exhort one another every day, as long as it is called "today," that none of you may be hardened by the deceitfulness of sin. For we have come to share in Christ, if indeed we hold our original confidence firm to the end. (3:12–14)

Unbelief leads us to fall away. Therefore, we need the exhortations of our brothers to fortify our hearts and give us courage, reminding us of our great reward, lest we be hardened by sin's lies. We must hold firm to our original confidence, standing firm in the evil day (as long as it is called "today") against danger, pain, and loss. Let us heed the example of those who fell away in unbelief and disobedience, and cling to Christ by faith as we strive to enter God's rest, enduring every hardship and trial that comes our way.

4

Biblical Boldness

HAVING CONSIDERED FAILURES of courage and examples of faintheartedness, we now consider examples of biblical boldness. What is biblical boldness? For some, the phrase conjures images of bravado, machismo, and swagger. For others, the phrase signifies a vague sense of courage and conviction in the face of opposition.

The fourth chapter of Acts provides an unusually clear picture of Christian boldness. The Greek noun for boldness (*parrēsia*) appears three times in this one chapter (and only twice more in the rest of Acts) and here sets the context for Luke's use of the verb meaning *speak boldly* (*parrēsiazomai*) seven times in the coming chapters. He apparently intends for us to see the events of this chapter as particularly poignant examples of Christian boldness. By examining these events, we can see not only what Christian boldness *is* but also where it comes from and how we can cultivate it for ourselves.

Astonished at Common Men

The word *boldness* first appears in Acts 4:13: "Now when they saw the boldness of Peter and John, and perceived that they were uneducated, common men, they were astonished." What have the Jewish leaders seen that so shocks them?

Recall that Peter and John are arrested following a miraculous healing at the temple (Acts 3:1–4:4). Peter has healed a man lame from birth, amazing the crowds. Peter follows the healing with an evangelistic sermon to the gathered crowd. The sermon is interrupted by the Jewish leaders, who—annoyed by the apostolic teaching—arrest the apostles and throw them in prison overnight.

The next day, Peter and John are brought before the entire council, including the high priest and his family. The rulers demand to know how Peter and John were able to do this miracle. And then Peter responds with the words that surprise the Sanhedrin and show us the meaning of boldness.

Three Elements of Christian Boldness

First, their boldness shines in a hostile context. The gathering of the entire council is undoubtedly an attempt to intimidate these uneducated, common fishermen. Here are the elite, the educated, the men who have power. It is they who basically ask, "What do you have to say for yourselves?"

No doubt other uneducated men have stood before them and shivered, looked pale, and found their tongues tied in the presence of these religious leaders. But not Peter and John. Their answer to the accusatory question is as clear as a bell: "Let it be known to all of you . . . ," Peter says (Acts 4:10). One imagines him lifting up his head and his voice so that he can be clearly heard by those in the back. This fisherman is unmoved in the presence of these leaders.

Second, their boldness manifests in their *clear* testimony about Jesus. It is by his name that the man was healed. It is by his name (and his name alone) that any man can be saved. This Jesus, whom God raised from the dead, is the cornerstone, and there is salvation in no one else (Acts 4:10–12). Thus, clarity about Jesus, and his power to heal and save, is at the heart of Christian boldness.

Finally, their boldness is displayed in their clarity about sin. This man, "Jesus Christ of Nazareth, *whom you crucified* . . . this Jesus is the stone that was rejected by you" (Acts 4:10–11). You rulers, you who purport to be the builders of Israel, rejected him, the cornerstone who has become for you a stone of stumbling and rock of offense. Here is a turning of the tables. Peter and John are the ones on trial; they have been arrested. And yet, here they accuse and condemn the powerful men who just a few months earlier killed Jesus himself.

So then, what is Christian boldness? It is courage and clarity about Jesus and sin in the face of powerful opposition. It is plain and open speech with no obfuscation or muttering. It is unhindered testimony to the truth, whether about Christ and his salvation or about what he came to save us from.

Obey God Rather Than Men

This understanding of boldness is confirmed if we consider the next chapter, where Peter and John are again arrested and hauled before these same leaders for their refusal to stop speaking in the name of Jesus.

The high priest questioned them, saying, "We strictly charged you not to teach in this name, yet here you have filled Jerusalem with your teaching, and you intend to bring this man's blood upon us." But Peter and the apostles answered, "We must obey God rather than men. The God of our fathers raised Jesus, whom you killed by hanging him on a tree. God exalted him at his right hand as Leader and Savior, to give repentance to Israel and forgiveness of sins. And we are witnesses to these things, and so is the Holy Spirit, whom God has given to those who obey him." (Acts 5:27–32)

"You have filled Jerusalem with your teaching." What teaching? The teaching about the resurrection of Jesus. The apostles are preaching the lordship of the risen Jesus with complete clarity and no hedging. "God exalted him at his right hand as Leader and Savior, to give repentance to Israel and forgiveness of sins" (Acts 5:31). That's what every sermon in Acts is about. God raised Jesus. God exalted Jesus. Jesus is Savior. Jesus is Lord. Jesus forgives sins. There is no other name by which we can be saved. This is the message the apostles preach in defiance of the Sanhedrin's threats. They are determined to fill Jerusalem with the good news about who Jesus is and what God has done through him.

But not only teaching about Jesus. They also preach clearly and courageously about sin—in particular, the sin of betraying, rejecting, denying, and murdering Jesus. "You intend to bring this man's blood upon us," the high priest says (Acts 5:28). In other words, "You're trying to blame us for killing him." "That's exactly right," responds Peter, in effect. "You killed [him] by hanging him on a tree" (Acts 5:30).

It's remarkable how often the apostles strike this note—in Jerusalem, no less, just months removed from the crucifixion itself. The unjust death of Jesus is fresh, and yet the apostles make it a repeated and central note in their preaching, both to the crowds and to the Jewish leaders:

> This Jesus, delivered up according to the definite plan and foreknowledge of God, *you crucified and killed by the hands of lawless men.* (Acts 2:23)

> God has made him both Lord and Christ, this Jesus *whom you crucified.* (Acts 2:36)

> The God of Abraham, the God of Isaac, and the God of Jacob, the God of our fathers, glorified his servant Jesus, *whom you delivered over and denied in the presence of Pilate,* when he had decided to release him. But you denied the Holy and Righteous One, and asked for a murderer to be granted to you, and *you killed the Author of life,* whom God raised from the dead. To this we are witnesses. (Acts 3:13–15)

> By the name of Jesus Christ of Nazareth, *whom you crucified*, whom God raised from the dead. . . . This Jesus is *the stone that was rejected by you, the builders.* (Acts 4:10–11)

And this clarity and courage about the particular sin of killing Jesus is one part of the larger apostolic clarity about all sin and the need to repent.

> Repent and be baptized every one of you in the name of Jesus Christ for the forgiveness of your sins, and you will receive the gift of the Holy Spirit. . . . Save yourselves from this crooked generation. (Acts 2:38, 40)

> Repent therefore, and turn back, that your sins may be blotted out. (Acts 3:19)

> God, having raised up his servant, sent him to you first, to bless you by turning every one of you from your wickedness. (Acts 3:26)

"Every one of you [turn] from *your* wickedness." Not your neighbor's wickedness. Not the wickedness of those people over there. Your wickedness. This is Christian boldness— clearly and courageously testifying to the resurrection of Jesus and the need to repent, both in general and in the specific ways that we have rebelled against God.

Dare to Be Specific

This leads us to a key lesson about Christian boldness. If we are to be bold, we must bring the reality of Jesus to bear on the reality of human sinfulness—and not just generic sinfulness. While calls for repentance from generic sins have their place, true Christian boldness gets specific about sin and particular about context.

There is a perennial temptation for Christian preachers to gather a crowd and preach about all the sins "out there." This could be preaching about sins out in the world. It could be preaching about sins present in other churches. But faithfulness and boldness demand that we address the sins actually present in whatever room we find ourselves. And if we ever wonder which sins we ought to boldly address, we can simply ask which sins we're tempted to ignore and minimize. Which sins do we tread lightly around? Where are we tempted to whisper? That context requires Christian boldness.

To put this another way, the preparation for boldness includes a growing self-awareness. We must learn to pay attention to our moments of reluctance, our hesitations, and our reactions. In other words, we must pay attention to our passions. These intuitive snap reactions are revealing; they are frequently attuned to our social context and tell us whom and what we fear. We must learn to interrogate our reluctance, to determine whether our hesitations are owing to wisdom and prudence or to cowardice and fear. If the latter, then this self-awareness enables us to fortify our minds and press through our natural reluctance in order to be bold.

And Peter and John maintain boldness in the face of threats and opposition as they go from being a mere nuisance (Acts 4:2), to the objects of jealousy (Acts 5:17), to the objects of rage and violence (Acts 5:33; 7:54). The opposition escalates, and the boldness abides.

Boldness in Preaching

Before turning to the source of such boldness, let's consider one more example, from later in the book of Acts. In Acts 21, Paul journeys to Jerusalem, compelled by the Holy Spirit, despite knowing that he is facing arrest, imprisonment, and likely death. When he arrives, he heeds the counsel of the apostle James and seeks to quell false rumors about his teaching by joining some Christian brothers in a ritual purification at the temple. While he is at the temple, Jews from Asia stir up a mob with false accusations: "This is the man who is teaching everyone everywhere against the people and the law and this place. Moreover, he even brought Greeks into the temple and has defiled this holy place" (21:28). (Paul has, in fact, not defiled the temple in this way.)

The mob starts to beat Paul, until Roman soldiers arrive and "rescue" him by arresting him. The Roman tribune mistakes Paul for an insurrectionist (21:38), and Paul corrects him and asks to address the people. We can already see Paul's composure and steadiness in the face of danger. The tribune sees a mob; Paul sees a congregation.

Paul's sermon to this crowd in Acts 22 is a wonderful combination of bridge building and boldness. On the one hand, he surprises the crowd by speaking to them in flawless Hebrew (they no doubt expected this antilaw, anti-Jew, Gentile-loving Christian to only speak Greek). He then gives his testimony and seeks to bridge the gap with his audience in order to lead them to Jesus:

- He emphasizes their shared Jewish heritage (22:3).
- He emphasizes their shared zeal for God ("as all of you are this day"—22:3).
- He emphasizes that he too persecuted Christians, dragging them to prison and even supervising executions (22:4–5).

He then describes his encounter with the risen Jesus on the road to Damascus. This is the turning point of his life, and his rhetorical strategy is obvious as he says, in effect: "I was a persecutor like you, zealous for God. And then Jesus knocked me off my horse and redirected my zeal. I'm still zealous for God, but my zeal is shaped and formed by the death and resurrection of the Messiah for my sins."

And then he continues to try to build bridges. He emphasizes that Ananias, the Christian who came to restore his sight and baptize him, was "a devout man according to the law, well spoken of by all the Jews" in Damascus (22:12). In the midst of this, he weaves in the gospel: Jesus is "the Righteous One" (22:14). When you call on his name, your sins are washed away (22:16). Baptism is the public identification with Jesus and his people. Paul even stresses that immediately after his conversion he came to the temple (which he allegedly opposes) in order to pray. In other words, his Christianity didn't lead him to turn away from Judaism; it fulfilled his Judaism.

So then, this is Paul the bridge builder essentially saying: "I was like you. I thought zeal for God meant opposing and persecuting followers of Jesus. But then my story collided with Jesus, and he changed everything. Well, not everything. I'm still zealous for God. Christians are devout people with good reputations. Because I called on the name of Jesus, the

Righteous One, my sins have been washed away. And yours can be too. You don't have to reject my testimony about Jesus."

But Paul knows that bridge building isn't enough, not if he is striving for Christian faithfulness. He must also be bold. He must show courage and clarity about Jesus and sin. Notice how Paul ends his sermon, and how the crowd reacts. "And he [Jesus] said to me, 'Go, for I will send you far away to the Gentiles.'" Up to this word they have listened to him. Now they raise their voices and say: "Away with such a fellow from the earth! For he should not be allowed to live" (22:21–22).

Take note that they have been listening to Paul; they've been eating it up. Some of them may begin to see themselves in Paul and be on their way to calling on Jesus. And then Paul spoils it by including the Gentiles in the people of God. At this, the crowd again goes ballistic, and the sermon is over.

There's no doubt that Paul knew what reaction his words were likely to get. This crowd was originally stirred up because they thought Paul brought a "dirty Gentile" into the temple (see Acts 21:28–29). Paul knows better than anyone that those zealous for the law can easily despise Gentiles. And yet, in his testimony, when he has the crowd hushed into silence listening to how Jesus changed his life, he includes the Gentiles anyway. He could've held off. He could have ended the sermon with "I was like you. Now you can be like me. Call on Jesus. He'll wash away your sins and purify your zeal for God." But he doesn't leave it there, because he can't leave it there. He has to be bold. He has to be clear and courageous about who Jesus is and what sin is.

And this is a challenging lesson for us. It's easy to want to preach the aspects of the gospel that people will like, to smooth over the rough edges so that we can win people to Jesus. "We'll talk about all the hard truths after they believe. We'll call that 'discipleship.' For now, we'll intentionally avoid any truths that we know will set them off."

But we may not do this. When we call people to repent of their sins and idolatries, we cannot avoid the ones that we know will make them angry. God sent Jesus to bless us by turning every one of us from our wickedness (Acts 3:26). *Our* wickedness. The particular wickedness that belongs to us. You can't preach the gospel to a white supremacist and not call him away from his racial pride and hatred. You can't preach the gospel to a partying frat guy and not call him away from his drunkenness and debauchery. You can't preach the gospel to a practicing homosexual and not call him away from practicing homosexuality. You can't preach the gospel to contemporary egalitarian progressives and not call them away from their commitment to a false view of human nature and marriage and men and women and sex.

Such preaching may end the relationship. People may say, "Away with such a bigot." But faithfulness to Jesus means that we don't have the right to adjust the truth to suit their sin. Our call is to testify to the truth, to witness to who Jesus is and what he has done. We hope and we pray that our witness and our testimony is persuasive, that God moves and that people embrace the good news. But our testimony and witness is faithful, whether it leads to conversion or to rejection. "We are the aroma of Christ . . . among those who are being saved and among those who are perishing" (2 Cor. 2:15)—the aroma of life to life and the aroma of death to death. So we cannot compromise, minimize, soften, or hide the truth in order to win converts. We must boldly bear witness, regardless of the response.

How Can We Grow in Courage?

Where then does this boldness come from? Fundamentally, it comes from the Holy Spirit. Peter, "filled with the Holy Spirit," answers the Sanhedrin's question (Acts 4:8). In the face of threats, the early Christians "were all filled with the Holy Spirit and continued to speak the word of God with boldness" (Acts 4:31). Stephen, "full of the Holy Spirit," indicts the Jewish leaders who have arrested and falsely accused him (Acts 7:55). As we saw in our reflections on Philippians 1, biblical courage is Spirit wrought and prayer fueled.

But not only the Holy Spirit. The Jewish leaders, in recognizing the apostolic boldness, recognize that Peter and John have "been with Jesus" (Acts 4:13). And while this no doubt refers to their engagement in Christ's earthly ministry, it contains a word for us today.

We too, if we wish to be bold, must be filled with the Spirit and abide with Jesus. And the book of Acts shows us not merely the ultimate source of Christian boldness but also the means for growing in it. After Peter and John are released and warned to no longer speak in the name of Jesus, what do they do?

First, they gather. "They went to their friends and reported what the chief priest and elders had said to them. And . . . they lifted their voices together" (Acts 4:23–24). Christian boldness is not an individualistic affair. It comes from gathering with God's people to seek his face together. As we saw in the last chapter, courage is contagious.

Second, they pray. "Sovereign Lord, who made the heaven and the earth and the sea and everything in them . . . look upon their threats and grant to your servants to continue to speak your word with all boldness" (Acts 4:24, 29). Boldness comes to those who ask the almighty Maker of heaven and earth for it. The Spirit fills them with Christian boldness because they petition the throne of grace to bestow it generously.

Paul requests precisely this type of prayer in the book of Ephesians. He asks the Ephesians to keep alert with perseverance and make supplication for him, "that words may be given to me in opening my mouth boldly to proclaim the mystery of the gospel, for which I am an ambassador in chains, that I may declare it boldly, as I ought to speak" (6:19–20). Paul ought to declare the gospel boldly, and he asks for prayer that God would supply what God demands.

Third, they ask God to make good on his promises. In their prayers, the saints in Acts repeat back to God what God has said. They quote Psalm 2 and celebrate God's royal victory in Jesus. Christian boldness is a boldness built on the word of God.

The opening exhortation in the book of Joshua underscores the biblical roots of boldness. The repeated exhortation to "be strong and courageous" is paired with an exhortation to meditate on the "Book of the Law" day and night, so that the word does not depart from our mouths (1:6, 8).

Finally, they look for God's hand and plan. Not only do they read the Bible and pray the Bible; they read their own story in light of the Scriptures, looking for God's hand and plan in their lives. They see God's providence behind the

Jewish and Roman opposition to Christ, and they see God's providence behind the continued opposition to Christ and his people.

The saints in Acts are not surprised by the fiery trial. They expect hardship and opposition. The scorn of men is not a shock to them. Jesus himself promised this sort of opposition.

And so neither should we be surprised. Instead we rest on his promises. He promised to be with us, to work for our good in all things, whether "distress, or persecution, or famine, or nakedness, or danger, or sword. . . . In all these things we are more than conquerors through him who loved us" (Rom. 8:35, 37).

Jesus's story is our story, and it is in the midst of that story that we gather and pray God's word in the Holy Spirit so that we, like the apostles, can speak God's word with boldness.

5

Courage and the Sexes

COURAGE HAS OFTEN BEEN REGARDED as a distinctly masculine virtue. Aristotle argued that the height of courage is the fortitude expressed in the face of death in battle. If war is necessary for the highest expression of courage, then of course courage will be closely linked to men, who are more often called to fight in wars.

Beyond the martial context, the association between men and courage owes in part to the predominant tendencies and dispositions of men and women. For example, men by nature are more prone to take risks and seek out danger voluntarily. As a result, they often find themselves in situations that call for risk-taking, daring, aggressive valor, and a pioneering spirit. Women, on the other hand, tend to be more risk averse, valuing security and safety more than men (though there are notable exceptions).

To put it more broadly, courage—the habitual self-possession and firmness of mind that overcomes fear through the power of a deeper desire for a greater good—takes many forms, in many different situations. Voluntarily seeking danger is not the only context for courage. Danger and hardship frequently find us, and they are no respecters of persons. Both men and women will find themselves confronting fighting without and fear within, and thus glad-hearted courage will be the order of the day.

So, certain forms of courage—such as daring or aggressive valor—will be more frequently displayed by men because men more often find themselves in situations that call for it. In other words, the link between men and these forms of courage is simply a matter of opportunity and context; women are clearly capable of such pioneering and voluntary risk-taking, even if they less often find themselves in situations that demand it. Thus, there is a *quantitative* dimension to the question of courage and the sexes, one which recognizes that because of their distinctive tendencies and callings, men and women will frequently display courage in different contexts.

But beyond this, we are still right to note distinctively masculine and feminine expressions of courage. That is, in addition to the quantitative dimension, there is also a *qualitative* dimension. Put simply, virtues are human. This means that, like so many aspects of our lives, they are both common to men and women *and* inflected by our sexuality. To inflect is to vary the pitch or tone of one's voice to express a particular mood or feeling. In grammar, to inflect is to change the form of a word to express a particular grammatical function or attribute, such as tense, mood, person, case, number, or gender.

For example, many languages (such as Spanish) have words that have masculine and feminine forms. *Hermano* means "brother"; *hermana* means "sister." *Hijo* means "son"; *hija* means "daughter." In both pairs, there is something common in the forms, something that indicates we are talking about siblings (*herman-*) or children (*hij-*). And yet, the ending of each word (the *o* and *a*) inflects the common element with the appropriate gender.

On this point, language reflects reality, including the reality of virtue. Virtues are common to humanity but inflected by sexuality. Courage is courage, whether in men or in women, whether risk-taking or endurance, whether aggressive valor or submissive fortitude. But because we are men and women all the way down, courage will always be embodied and expressed in distinctly masculine and feminine ways.

As always, such definitions can be a bit abstract. Stories often communicate such realities with more clarity and concreteness. In the remainder of this chapter, I'll attempt to capture both the quantitative and the qualitative dimensions of courage in men and women by highlighting examples of courageous men and women—first in the Bible, then in Shakespeare, and then in Narnia. My hope is that these examples might inspire all Christians to embody such courage in their own lives.

Take Courage and Be Men

The Scriptures give us many examples of masculine courage, some of which we have seen in previous chapters. Some passages explicitly link courage with masculinity. In 1 Samuel 4, the Philistines make war on Israel. The Israelites are defeated and attempt to explain their loss. They realize that they did not bring the ark of the covenant up with them to battle, and so they call the priests to bring it into the camp, essentially treating the ark like a magic talisman.

When the Philistines hear that the ark is in the camp, they quake with fear. They have heard what the God of the Hebrews did to the Egyptians, and they fear lest the same thing happen to them. Nevertheless, they encourage one another, saying, "Take courage, and be men, O Philistines, lest you become slaves to the Hebrews as they have been to you; be men and fight" (1 Sam. 4:9). Taking courage, being a man, and fighting in battle are all inextricably linked. (And because of Israel's faithlessness, the Philistines again prevail over them in battle.)

Later in 1 Samuel, we see the classic instance of biblical courage among the Israelites. Goliath of Gath is the great Philistine warrior—towering in height, massive in strength, battle-tested, and well armed. He defies the armies of Israel and challenges them to single combat. His stature, his strength, his scorn, and his skill intimidate the men of Israel. King Saul and all Israel are "dismayed and greatly afraid" (17:11). The passion of fear overwhelms them, and they flee (17:24).

Young David, the shepherd, youngest son of Jesse, visits his older brothers in the Israelite camp. He hears Goliath's mockery and defiance. He recognizes the reproach that has fallen upon Israel because of their fear. By fleeing from the Philistine, Israel suffers shame and humiliation. David is shocked by their unmanly cowardice and volunteers to fight Goliath. "Let no man's heart fail because of [Goliath]. Your servant will go and fight with this Philistine" (17:32). Note that David's courage is expressed in a willingness, even an eagerness, to fight a formidable enemy.

When King Saul protests that David is too young to fight such a battle, David reminds him that shepherds must learn courage and violence from a young age in order to protect their flocks from lions and bears. In describing his bravery and experience, David perfectly expresses the paradox of biblical courage. On the one hand, *David* is the one who struck the lion and delivered the lamb from its mouth. David has struck down both lions and bears, and therefore will also strike down the uncircumcised Philistine who defies the armies of the living God (17:34–37). On the other hand, David acknowledges that it was not his own strength and prowess at work, but the Lord himself. "The LORD who delivered me from the paw of the lion and from the paw of the bear will deliver me from the hand of this Philistine" (17:37). David's courage is grounded in the Lord's strength and favor.

David shows the same biblical courage to Goliath himself. In the face of the giant's taunts, David says: "You come to me with a sword and with a spear and with a javelin, but I come to you in the name of the LORD of hosts, the God of the armies of Israel, whom you have defied. This day the LORD will deliver you into my hand, and I will strike you down and cut off your head" (17:45–46). The Lord will deliver Goliath into David's hand. But David is active as well. He will strike down Goliath. That's what it means to courageously fight in the name of the Lord. Again, the form of courage is aggressive, risk-taking, and martial, expressed in combat and struggle.

Once More unto the Breach

Our books, plays, and movies are filled with scenes like the battle of David and Goliath. From *Braveheart* to *Gladiator* to *The Lord of the Rings*, men resonate with the moment in the movie when the battle lines are drawn up and the leader stands before his troops in order to strengthen their resolve and fan their courage into flame. Such scenes typically end with the leader charging into battle at the head of his men, exercising martial bravery and valor.

Shakespeare's *Henry V* contains a classic example of such a scene. King Henry leads his men against the French armies in a quest to claim his throne. He besieges the city of Harfleur and utters one of the most famous battle speeches in literature.[1] In doing so, he expresses and embodies many of the truths we've seen about courage:

Once more unto the breach, dear friends, once more;
Or close the wall up with our English dead!

[1] William Shakespeare, *Henry V*, act 3, scene 1, https://www.poetryfoundation .org/. To see a fantastic performance of this speech, search for the video of Jamie Parker as King Henry at the Globe Theatre in London.

Courage doesn't quit. Once more, once more. Again, again. Here is the fortitude and endurance that is the mark of courage, even to death.

> In peace there's nothing so becomes a man
> As modest stillness and humility:
> But when the blast of war blows in our ears,
> Then imitate the action of the tiger;

There are certain virtues appropriate for peacetime. Modesty, humility, calmness, tranquility—all of these have their place. But when war comes, men must rise to something else. They must imitate the action of the tiger. Or as the Bible says, "The righteous are as bold as a lion" (Prov. 28:1). How do we imitate the tiger?

> Stiffen the sinews, summon up the blood,
> Disguise fair nature with hard-favour'd rage;
> Then lend the eye a terrible aspect;
> Let pry through the portage of the head
> Like the brass cannon; let the brow o'erwhelm it
> As fearfully as doth a galled rock
> O'erhang and jutty his confounded base,
> Swill'd with the wild and wasteful ocean.

Now set the teeth and stretch the nostril wide,
Hold hard the breath and bend up every spirit
To his full height.

The whole body is engaged in this imitation. Facial expressions, furrowed brows, piercing eyes of rage, clenched teeth, flared nostrils, muscles taut and ready to pounce. Henry's speech gives his men a model to emulate:

On, on, you noblest English.
Whose blood is fet from fathers of war-proof!
Fathers that, like so many Alexanders,
Have in these parts from morn till even fought
And sheathed their swords for lack of argument:
Dishonour not your mothers; now attest
That those whom you call'd fathers did beget you.
Be copy now to men of grosser blood,
And teach them how to war.

Here Henry speaks to the noblemen of England. Not only should they imitate a tiger ready to spring for his prey; they must also imitate their warlike ancestors. These ancestors were battle-tested and proved. Like Alexander the Great, they fought from dawn till dusk, from sunrise to sunset, until there was no one left to fight. The call to courage is a call to live up to the honor and glory of their fathers and mothers. Courage is about bearing their ancestral names well, living up to the reputation that has been left to them.

More than that, the noble English are to spread their courage to the commoners and teach them how to war.

> And you, good yeoman,
> Whose limbs were made in England, show us here
> The mettle of your pasture; let us swear
> That you are worth your breeding; which I doubt not;
> For there is none of you so mean and base,
> That hath not noble lustre in your eyes.

Finally, Henry calls the commoners to rise to the glory of their country. No matter how common or low their birth, Henry sees a nobility in their eyes. They are Englishmen, valiant and bold.

> I see you stand like greyhounds in the slips,
> Straining upon the start. The game's afoot:
> Follow your spirit, and upon this charge
> Cry "God for Harry, England, and Saint George!"

Here is the final call, the final en*courage*ment, in which Henry utters his war cry, reminds his men of the God and good for which they fight, and leads his men once more unto the breach. His courage is manifested in a kind of aggressive valor, a willingness to take risks and overcome obstacles on the way to achieving the goal of victory. This courage is contagious, spreading from Henry to his noblemen and from them to the common soldiers. Henry's words and actions fortify his men so they can overcome their fear and fight with a kind of intensity and abandon that will carry them to victory.

First in, Last out, Laughing Loudest

Speeches like Henry's have echoed down through our stories for the last four hundred years. I suspect that Shakespeare's portrayal of Henry influenced Lewis's description of kingship in *The Horse and His Boy*. Here is how King Lune expresses the heart of kingship to his sons:

> For this is what it means to be a king: to be first in every desperate attack and last in every desperate retreat, and when there's hunger in the land (as must be now and then in bad years) to wear finer clothes and laugh louder over a scantier meal than any man in your land.[2]

2   C. S. Lewis, *The Horse and His Boy* (New York: HarperCollins, 2009), 185.

Make no mistake; these are no mere words. King Lune backs them up with action. When the gates of Anvard open during the battle with Rabadash, Lune is the first one to face the foe. He knows deep in his heart that to be a leader means that you have the privilege of dying first.

But kingship isn't merely about battle and war. It's also about leadership in the midst of other trials (such as famine). What's more, we must not miss Lewis's emphasis on laughter as a key element of courageous kingship. Courage doesn't face hardship with dour resolution and resignation. Courage laughs loudest in the midst of the trial. David gestures toward this picture of courage in Psalm 19:5–6 when he compares the blazing sun, as it moves across the sky, to a warrior who runs his course *with joy*. Picture Josheb-basshebeth, one of David's mighty men, running into battle with spear raised and eyes aflame with purpose and joy.

Courage is a kind of glad-hearted stability and manifest hopefulness in the face of hardship. Lewis elsewhere identifies laughter and gaiety and wholeheartedness as "the natural accompaniment of courage,"[3] whether in war or elsewhere. The danger is real, the fear may be palpable, but true courage

3   C. S. Lewis, *Mere Christianity* (New York: HarperCollins, 2001), 119.

is all in, wholehearted, and therefore rejoices in the labor to overcome every obstacle.

Because both courage and fear are contagious, a leader knows that there are times when he must put on the brave face, when he must en*courage* those in his care by open expressions of hopefulness and joy. One thinks of Jimmy Braddock in the movie *Cinderella Man*, giving his still-hungry daughter his own breakfast, on the grounds that he had dreamt of a steak dinner and was still full.

Or of Roberto Benigni's portrayal of Guido Orefice in *Life Is Beautiful*. Guido, an Italian Jew, and his family are sent to a concentration camp during the Holocaust. In order to preserve his young son's innocence in the face of the evil, Guido pretends that the whole thing is a game, telling his son, Giosue, that in order to earn a thousand points and win a tank, he must not cry or complain. Guido maintains the game throughout the movie, even to the end, when a German officer leads him to his execution while Giosue hides in a box. Guido playfully marches past the box and winks at his son, in effect laughing loudest for his son's good, even in the face of horrors.

Such are images of masculine courage in the face of war, death, and hardship. As those called to lead others in the home, the church, and the world, men need such models of joyful sacrifice, glad-hearted valor, pioneering risk-taking, and intense but happy daring in whatever calling God gives them. And so may God grant us the grace to rise to the courageous spirit of King Lune—first in, last out, and laughing loudest.

Holy Women Who Hope in God

Among the Greeks, courage and fortitude were especially masculine virtues, since the pinnacle of the virtue involved physical strength and aggressive valor in battle. Christianity transformed the classical virtue by elevating the endurance of suffering and evil as the pinnacle of fortitude. Martyrdom, more than aggression in battle, became the clearest expression of Christian fortitude.

This shift in emphasis and focus allows us to see expressions of courage in other places. Courage is no longer merely the province of strong, able-bodied men. Women, children, and the weak are able to cultivate and display Christian courage in their stability of soul and patient endurance of evil.

The apostle Peter expresses precisely this view of courage in his exhortation to Christian wives. Wives are to be subject to their husbands, even when their husbands are unbelieving and disobedient. Rather than adorning themselves externally with the physical trappings of beauty, they are to adorn themselves with "the imperishable beauty of a gentle and quiet spirit, which in God's sight is very precious" (1 Pet. 3:4).

"A gentle and quiet spirit" is not a personality trait (as though God prefers introverts to extroverts). There's nothing inherently virtuous in being a shy wallflower. Instead, "a gentle and quiet spirit" refers to mental fortitude, emotional strength, and spiritual composure. This sort of woman has a well-ordered soul, one that is composed and content in her calling and station.

A quiet spirit is the opposite of a loud one. Consider Solomon's warnings about the forbidden woman, the adulteress:

> She is loud and wayward;
>   her feet do not stay at home. (Prov. 7:11)

The apostle Paul issues a similar warning about women who are "idlers, going about from house to house, and not only idlers, but also gossips and busybodies, saying what they should not" (1 Tim. 5:13). The opposite of such loud, discontented, wayward women are those who "marry, bear children, manage their households, and give the adversary no occasion for slander" (1 Tim. 5:14).

Peter goes on to explicitly link the "gentle and quiet spirit" of 1 Peter 3:4 with submission to one's husband: "For this is how the holy women who hoped in God used to adorn themselves, by submitting to their own husbands, as Sarah obeyed Abraham, calling him lord" (1 Pet. 3:5–6). In verse 4, the adornment is the gentle and quiet spirit. In verse 5, it's Sarah-like submission to one's husband. And then in verse 6, Peter connects all of this to courage. "And you are her children, if you do good and *do not fear anything that is frightening*."

This passage then confirms and expands the vision of courage that has been presented throughout this book. Drawing the various elements in the passage together, we see that Sarah is presented as a model of courage. Sarah's children "do not fear anything that is frightening." Courage here is a matter of inner fortitude and mental strength. Before it ever expresses itself in action, it resides in "the hidden person of the heart."

This inner strength comes from a vibrant and living hope in God. Like Joshua and the people of Israel, Sarah and her daughters must be strong and courageous because they know and believe that God is with them and for them. What's more, such hope in God firmly believes that hardship, trials, and dangers are instruments in the hands of God for our good. Such hope clings to God and thereby subdues the passions of fear and anxiety about the future.

The link between holiness, hope, and courage recalls an earlier passage, 1 Peter 1:13–16, where Peter writes:

> Therefore, preparing your minds for action, and being sober-minded, set your hope fully on the grace that will be brought to you at the revelation of Jesus Christ. As obedient children, do not be conformed to the passions of your former ignorance, but as he who called you is holy, you also be holy in all your conduct, since it is written, "You shall be holy, for I am holy." (1 Pet. 1:13–16)

Notice the three phrases in verse 13: (1) "preparing your minds for action," (2) "being sober-minded," and (3) "set your hope fully on the grace that will be brought to you."

The first phrase literally means "girding up the loins of your mind." To use a modern image, we might say, "rolling up the sleeves of your mind." Peter calls his readers to get ready to do some serious mental work, the kind that takes effort. This isn't roll-out-of-bed-in-your-pajamas work. This is put-on-your-work-clothes, make-sure-your-shoes-are-tied, get-your-game-face-on work.

The second phrase refers to the opposite of drunkenness. Be sober-minded. Now, drunkenness impairs our perception, our judgment, our reaction times. So the opposite of drunkenness is an alertness, a clarity of mind, a steadiness. So roll up the sleeves of your mind, get clear and steady, and then what?

The final phrase calls for a particular affectionate response. Hope is a future-oriented affection. It is a glad-hearted expectation of something good that is coming. We don't yet possess it; we don't hope for what we already have. And Peter knows it is far too easy to be distracted by the cares and anxieties of this world—to look to the future with fear rather than faith.

And so he exhorts us: Roll up the sleeves of your minds, get clear and steady, and then set your hope fully on the grace that will be brought to you. You've been born again to a living hope, an imperishable inheritance (1 Pet. 1:3–5). Now set your hope fully on the tidal wave of coming grace.

Peter goes on to ground such hope-filled and holy obedience in the gospel—Christ has ransomed us with his precious blood, and through him we are believers in God "so that [our] faith and hope are in God" (1 Pet. 1:17–21).

Sarah, then, is a model (for both men and women) of this kind of sober-minded, hope-filled obedience to lawful authority. Her gentle and quiet spirit isn't a matter of personality or simple resignation. It took grace-wrought effort to subdue her fears because it is a fearful thing to submit to a fallible man. When we consider Sarah's life—following Abram when God called him to leave Ur; the perpetual risk of tyrannical kings who sought to add her to their harems; danger from local warlords, like those who captured Lot and his family—we can more deeply appreciate that she faced many frightening things. And yet, because of her hope in God, she conquered such fears and maintained a gentle and quiet spirit, a sober-minded spirit in submission first to God and then to her husband.

And here we see the way that Sarah's femininity inflected her courage. Her courage did not manifest as the aggressive valor of the warrior. When Lot and his family were captured, Sarah did not join with Abram and his 318 warriors to rescue them. Instead, her courage expressed itself in glad submission to her husband. She honored him by her speech ("calling him lord") and her actions.

And it's significant that Peter highlights her use of the term "lord" in Genesis 18:12. "So Sarah laughed to herself, saying, 'After I am worn out, and my lord is old, shall I have pleasure?'" What's remarkable about Peter's citation is how unremarkable the term is in the passage. This seems to simply be the way Sarah talked about her husband. Calling him lord testifies that she was a great and holy woman, one who hoped in God, honored her husband, and thereby became a model of Christian courage.

Wisdom and Courage

Sarah is not the only female example of courage in the Bible. We might also consider Jael, the wife of Heber the Kenite, who drives a tent peg through the skull of the Canaanite commander oppressing Israel in Judges 4. Her valor is inflected with feminine shrewdness and maternal guile as she invites Sisera into her tent, offers him milk, and tucks him into bed before crushing his skull with a hammer and peg.

Even more than this, we might consider Abigail, the wise and discerning wife of the foolish Nabal. After her husband wickedly insults David (despite David's protection of Nabal's flocks), David succumbs to rash anger and plans to strike Nabal's entire household.

Hearing of her husband's insult and the evil that is coming to their house, Abigail takes responsibility for her household in the face of her husband's folly. But, like Sarah in the story of Abraham and the kings, she does not do so by taking up the sword to defend her people. Instead, she shows the same gentle and quiet spirit that hopes in God and does not fear.

She immediately prepares a lavish gift of food and wine for David and his men. She brings the gifts and falls on her face before David and pleads for his favor. She testifies to her husband's folly. She gives David the gifts. But most importantly, she makes two fundamental appeals. First, she urges David to refrain from shedding innocent blood and working salvation with his own hand (1 Sam. 25:26). By refraining from these things, he will avoid the grief and pangs of conscience that will come if he brings bloodguilt by his hand or seeks to save himself (1 Sam. 25:31). Second, she reminds David that the Lord will fight for him, that David's life is "bound in the bundle of the living in the care of the LORD your God" (1 Sam. 25:29).

These appeals check the rashness of the king. They arrest his rage and wrath and vengeance. They enable him to tame the passion of his impulsive anger. David blesses Abigail for her discretion and courage because she has "kept me this day from bloodguilt and from working salvation with my own hand" (1 Sam. 25:33). And he blesses the Lord, who sent her to him and restrained David's hand from doing great evil by harming Abigail and her husband's household.

And sure enough, the Lord vindicates David. Ten days later, the Lord strikes Nabal to his death, avenging the insult against his anointed (1 Sam. 25:38–39). Not only does David spare himself from working evil; he gains the hand of a wise, discerning, and courageous wife.

Hermione and Paulina

In Shakespeare's romance *The Winter's Tale*, we see Sarah-like fortitude and Abigail-like bravery in the characters of Hermione and her friend Paulina. Hermione is the pregnant queen of Sicilia, married to King Leontes. Leontes's close friend Polixenes, king of Bohemia, has been visiting his friends for nine months. In a fit of feverish jealousy, Leontes comes to suspect that Polixenes has cuckolded him and fathered the child in Hermione's womb.

Though Leontes's suspicions are actually false, Polixenes flees in fear, strengthening Leontes's accusations. He vents his rage on Hermione, throwing her into prison while he waits for confirmation of her guilt from the oracle at Delphos. When the child is born, Hermione's friend Paulina boldly brings her to the king, hoping to soften his wrath.

Leontes attempts to cast Paulina from his presence, but she bravely insists on remaining and speaking the truth. In doing so, she shows more courage than the cowardly nobles of the Bohemian court, who—despite their disbelief in the accusations—will not openly oppose the king.

Paulina says that she brings tiding from the "good queen."[4] Leontes dismisses such language with a scoff. Paulina resolutely doubles and triples down:

4   William Shakespeare, *The Winter's Tale*, act 2, scene 3, https://shakespeare.folger.edu/.

Good queen, my lord, good queen, I say "good queen,"
And would by combat make her good, so were I
A man.

Leontes repeatedly tries to banish her, but Paulina will not relent. She shows him the child, who clearly looks like the king. The king persists in his wrath, denouncing the child as a bastard and his court as a nest of traitors. Paulina turns the accusation around, declaring that the only traitor present is Leontes

himself. For he
The sacred honor of himself, his queen's,
His hopeful son's, his babe's, betrays to slander.

Leontes erupts, calls for the child to be killed, and threatens to burn Paulina alive. But, in the face of this imminent danger, Paulina continues to speak the truth and intercede for her friend and the baby:

I'll not call you tyrant;
But this most cruel usage of your queen,
Not able to produce more accusation
Than your own weak-hinged fancy, something savors

Of tyranny, and will ignoble make you,
Yea, scandalous to the world.

As in Abigail, here we see feminine courage, not in combat as a man, but as a faithful intercessor who refuses to be silent in the face of outrageous injustice, despite threats to her life.

When Hermione is brought to trial, we see a glorious picture of courage as she endures hardship. She entrusts herself to "powers divine," which "behold our human actions" and judge rightly. She asserts her innocence of the charge of infidelity, pointing to her years of faithfulness and glad submission to her husband (whom she continues to address as "my lord"). She confesses that she loved and honored Polixenes as was appropriate for a queen to love her husband's closest friend. And having clung to the truth, she disdains death and all the pleasures of life and commits herself to the judgment of the gods.

In both Paulina and Hermione, then, we see the imperishable beauty of a gentle and quiet spirit. Their gentleness is not passivity, and a quiet spirit does not keep them from speaking the truth. But they are composed and gracious; they have girded up the loins of their minds, and they cling to what is true and right in the face of every earthly pressure and danger. They refuse to shrink back in fear or remain silent

COURAGE AND THE SEXES

in cowardice. Like Sarah and Abigail, they set their hope on things above and seek to do good, not fearing anything that is frightening.

The Courage of a Narnian Queen

Turning finally to Narnia, we see a similar picture of feminine courage. Queen Lucy is called the Valiant, but her bravery is not primarily courage in battle.[5] As Father Christmas says, "Battles are ugly when women fight." Nevertheless, he does give Lucy and Susan weapons, but instructs them to use them "only in great need."[6] The point is this: unless there is no choice, it is unseemly for women to fight in battle. However, in emergencies—such as when an army makes a surprise attack on an ally (as in *The Horse and His Boy*), or when there are only a handful of faithful Narnians fighting dozens of Calormenes and traitors (as in *The Last Battle*)—women too can show themselves valiant in war. But this is not the primary way that female courage is displayed.

Instead, the courage of a Narnian queen is displayed in her glad-hearted submission to authority. When Edmund

---

5　See Joe Rigney, *Live Like a Narnian: Christian Discipleship in Lewis's Chronicles* (Minneapolis: Eyes & Pen, 2013), 155–57.

6　C. S. Lewis, *The Lion, the Witch and the Wardrobe* (New York: HarperCollins, 2009), 108–9.

begins to quarrel with Peter in *Prince Caspian*, Lucy whispers to him, "Hadn't we better do what Peter says? He is the High King, you know."[7] Lucy knows that obedience to Aslan often includes deference, honor, and submission to those whom he appoints over us. In this way, she is a model of submission for all men and women who are under authority.

At the same time, Lucy is willing to disobey Peter later in the story, when she has been given clear instructions from Aslan to follow, whether the others do or not. Lucy knows that ultimately she must obey Aslan, not man (high king or otherwise). What's more, she must show courage in one of the most difficult circumstances by being willing to displease those closest to her.

Examples of the courage of a Narnian queen abound in the stories. Aravis is described as "true as steel" and would never dream of deserting a companion, whether she liked him or not (*The Horse and His Boy*, chap. 6). She maintains her composure when her friend Lasaraleen is overtaken by fear after overhearing the Tisroc's evil plans. Lucy's courage wins the admiration of Caspian and the rest when she volunteers to venture into the magician's house on behalf of the Monopods (*The Voyage of the Dawn Treader*, chap. 9). Polly

7   C. S. Lewis, *Prince Caspian* (New York: HarperCollins, 2009), 88.

shows herself to be a true, faithful, and courageous friend to Digory when she asks to travel with him on his errand to the west (*The Magician's Nephew*, chap. 12).

In all of these cases, whether in the Bible, in Shakespeare, or in Narnia, we see the inner strength and patient fortitude that God regards as very precious. Courage is human—common to both sexes—and yet inflected in masculine and feminine ways. And whatever form it takes, true courage, grounded by hope in God, subduing internal fears and facing external dangers, is a wonderful and beautiful thing.

Conclusion

THIS BOOK BEGAN BY REFLECTING on Philippians 1, a passage about danger and fear, boldness and courage. I want to end it with an exhortation from Psalm 27, a song about danger and fear, boldness and courage. The opening verse of the psalm contains a question:

> Whom shall I fear? . . .
> Of whom shall I be afraid?

The psalm describes the various dangers that David is facing. David has enemies, adversaries, and foes (27:2, 11–12). Evildoers assail him in order to devour him (27:2). An army encamps against him; war is coming (27:3). False witnesses slander him, breathing violence and lies in order to ruin him. What's more, David's family has forsaken him;

his earthly supports are gone. David is facing days of danger and distress. So when David asks, "Whom shall I fear?" the answer is obvious: Your enemies, your adversaries, your foes, David. You are facing the loss of your reputation, bodily harm, and potential death. Fear is the most natural thing in the world.

And yet David does not fear. He is confident and terror-proof. Despite the external dangers and absence of earthly support, his heart is not agitated or distressed. He is steadfast and full of courage. Why?

Because the Lord is his light in the darkness. The Lord is his salvation and rescue. The Lord is the stronghold and refuge of his life (27:1). God will lead David on a level path so as to avoid the traps and snares set for him (27:11). David is confident that God will deal with his enemies. They will stumble and fall into their own traps (27:2). God will hide David from the trouble. David uses layered images to make God's deliverance and protection concrete: God will hide him in his shelter, conceal him in his tent, lift him up on a rock. And from that high vantage, David will look in triumph on his enemies and worship God with joy and gladness (27:6). He is confident that he will look upon the Lord "in the land of the living" (27:13).

In other words, David's question—"Whom shall I fear?"—is the same one that Paul asks in Romans 8:31: "If God is for us, who can be against us?" And the answer is: everyone . . . and no one. Everyone, because there are enemies and dangers. No one, because none of these enemies and dangers can succeed against us. None of them can triumph over us. As David says elsewhere:

> This I know, that God is for me.
> In God, whose word I praise,
>   in the Lord, whose word I praise,
> in God I trust; I shall not be afraid.
>   What can man do to me? (Ps. 56:9–11)

How can we have such confidence that no enemy can prevail against us? Because God "did not spare his own Son but gave him up for us all," so that he can freely and graciously give us everything (Rom. 8:32). No one can "bring any charge against God's elect" and make it stick (Rom. 8:33). God will not cast us away in his anger (Ps. 27:9) because Christ Jesus has died for us; more than that, has been raised for us; more than that, is seated at God's right hand as our intercessor. Because of him, we can be confident that we will look upon the Lord in the land of the living, in the realm of the resurrection.

No danger can separate us from God's love. Not "tribulation, or distress, or persecution, or famine, or nakedness, or danger, or sword" (Rom. 8:35). In fact, all of these dangers, which could conceivably crush us with fear, are now instruments in God's hands. In them, "we are more than conquerors through him who loved us" (Rom. 8:37). Paul and David have the same conviction: God is for them, and therefore they need not fear.

But perhaps more striking than David's confidence in God's protection and deliverance is the one thing he wants in the meantime. What steels David's nerves in the moment, what fortifies his heart in the face of danger is one thing.

One thing have I asked of the LORD,
    that will I seek after:
that I may dwell in the house of the LORD
    all the days of my life,
to gaze upon the beauty of the LORD
    and to inquire in his temple. (Ps. 27:4)

This is David's great hope: dwelling in God's presence and gazing on his beauty forever. This is what anchors David when the nations rage and the enemies prowl and the earth gives way and the waters foam.

God has called David to seek his face. David has answered that call: "Your face, LORD, do I seek" (Ps. 27:8). And God's face is enough for David.

And it is enough for us. At the end of Psalm 27, David invites us to join him in his courage. "Wait for the LORD," he says.

> Be strong, and let your heart take courage;
> wait for the LORD! (27:14)

In other words, be fortified by the conviction that God will take you in when you are cast out. Strengthen your mind and steady your soul by the truth that God will give you himself forever. In the words of Jesus, "In the world, you will have tribulation. But take heart; I have overcome the world" (John 16:33).

Acknowledgments

SMALL BOOKS ARE STILL the fruit of great grace. Time would fail me to acknowledge all those who have had a hand in shaping this small book. Nevertheless, gratitude is a debt that I'm happy to pay.

For my friend Mike Reeves, who graciously invited me to contribute to this series.

For Thom Notaro, who smoothed out my prose and posed good questions that improved the content.

For the team at Crossway for making book writing (and editing, and marketing) a joy.

For the faculty at Bethlehem College and Seminary and pastors at Cities Church, who have encouraged and challenged me in more ways than I can count.

For friends like Andy and Jenni Naselli, Tom and Abigail Dodds, and David Mathis, who all read portions of this book and gave valuable feedback along the way.

For Clint Manley, who did a deep edit of an early draft and helped me to fill out some of the content.

For my sons—Sam, Peter, and Jack—who by God's grace inspire me to face my fears and master my passions so that I can help them to become men of courage and fortitude. Nothing produces courage as much as having something worthwhile to fight for.

For my wife, Jenny, who encourages me daily to be the kind of glad-hearted, steady, bold, and courageous man that God wants me to be.

If I have one main hope for this book, it's that the quality of courage comes through its pages—that readers not just find definitions and descriptions but really feel the wonder of joyful stability, mental fortitude, and emotional strength that takes risks, faces danger, and overcomes fear by the power of a deeper desire for the greatest good. That quality has come to me in many forms, from King David to King Lune, from the apostle Paul to Mr. Latimer and Mr. Ridley.

But in terms of personal acquaintance, no one has imparted the quality of happy courage to me more than my friend Doug Wilson. For over fifteen years, I've benefited from his glad-hearted steadfastness, hopeful stability, and cheerful ministry, and my prayer is that some element of that quality comes through in these pages.

Bibliography

Chesterton, G. K. *Orthodoxy*. Chicago: Moody Publishers, 2009. Kindle. First published 1908.

Edwards, Jonathan. *Ethical Writings*, edited by Paul Ramsey. Vol. 8 of *The Works of Jonathan Edwards*. New Haven, CT: Yale University Press, 1989.

Lewis, C. S. *The Abolition of Man*. New York: HarperCollins, 2001. First published 1943.

Lewis, C. S. *The Horse and His Boy*. New York: HarperCollins, 2009. First published 1954.

Lewis, C. S. *The Lion, the Witch and the Wardrobe*. New York: HarperCollins, 2009. First published 1950.

Lewis, C. S. *Mere Christianity*. New York: HarperCollins, 2001. First published 1943.

Lewis, C. S. *Prince Caspian*. New York: HarperCollins, 2009. First published 1951.

Lewis, C. S. *The Screwtape Letters*. New York: HarperCollins, 2001. First published 1942.

Rigney, Joe. *Live Like a Narnian: Christian Discipleship in Lewis's Chronicles*. Minneapolis: Eyes & Pen, 2013.

General Index

preaching clearly and courageously about, 77–79
sober-mindedness, 107–8
Solomon, 48, 51
speaking boldly, 73
spies, fear of people of the land,
63–64
"standing firm," 31
Stephen, 86
stewards of God's grace, 20
"stiff-necked" people, 64
"striving together," 31
submission to one's husband,
105–6, 109–10
suffering for Jesus, 12
superior desire, 32
superior fear, 32

Tao, 24–25
temperance, 17
throne of grace, 40
timidity, 57
tranquility, 98
true virtues, 18–19

unbelief, 64, 65, 70, 72
union with Christ, 12, 19

unity, relentless labor and pursuit
of, 11

valor in battle, 104
value, 25–26
vice, 57–58
virtue, 17–21
inflected in masculine and
feminine ways, 93
and vice, 57–58
Voyage of the Dawn Treader, The
(Lewis), 116

waiting for the Lord, 123
way of life, 10–11
Wesley, Charles, 43–44
white supremacy, 85
wickedness, 85
will, 28
Winter's Tale, The (Shakespeare),
112–15
wisdom, 17, 31
women
Christian courage of, 104
as risk averse, 91
worthy life, 10–11
wrath of God, 37–38, 39

Scripture Index

Union

We fuel reformation in churches and lives.

Union Publishing invests in the next generation of leaders with theology that gives them a taste for a deeper knowledge of God. From books to our free online content, we are committed to producing excellent resources that will refresh, transform, and grow believers and their churches.

We want people everywhere to know, love, and enjoy God, glorifying him in everything they do. For this reason, we've collected hundreds of free articles, podcasts, book chapters, and video content for our free online collection. We also produce a fresh stream of written, audio, and video resources to help you to be more fully alive in the truth, goodness, and beauty of Jesus.

If you are hungry for reformational resources that will help you delight in God and grow in Christ, we'd love for you to visit us at unionpublishing.org.

unionpublishing.org

Also Available in the Growing Gospel Integrity Series

This series invites readers to pursue spiritual growth through four marks of integrity: worthy lives, unity, courage, and humility. Each book examines one of these marks—why they are essential, what they should look like, how the gospel molds these qualities, and how individuals and churches can be shaped by them. Through this series, Christians will be challenged to grow in spiritual integrity, rejoicing in and living by the gospel they profess.

For more information, visit **crossway.org**.